D1042160

I DO IT WITH THE LIGHTS ON

I DO IT WITH THE LIGHTS ON

And 10 More Discoveries on the Road
to a Blissfully Shame-Free Life

WHITNEY WAY THORE

Ballantine Books
New York

Copyright © 2016 by Whitney Way Thore

Published in the United States by Ballantine Books,
an imprint of Random House, a division of
Penguin Random House LLC, New York.

BALLANTINE and the HOUSE colophon are registered trademarks
of Penguin Random House LLC.

ISBN 978-0-399-59450-2
ebook ISBN 978-0-399-59451-9

Printed in the United States of America on acid-free paper

randomhousebooks.com

246897531

First Edition

Book design by Virginia Norey

For my heroes:
Mom, Dad, and Hunter

And for anyone who needs proof
that life gets lighter, brighter, and better

Contents

I DO IT WITH THE LIGHTS ON

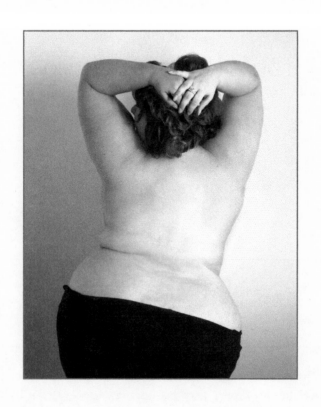

1

LIFE GOT BETTER
WHEN I WAS FAT

I t was the sexiest photo I'd ever taken.

At 340 pounds, I was only just beginning to believe such a thing was possible. It was the fall of 2013 and a local photographer had asked me to pose seminude for a boudoir photo shoot. I was the heaviest I'd ever been, and in real danger of being the most miserable I'd ever been, when I decided to approach my life in a different way. I promised myself that instead of declining an opportunity on the basis of my body insecurity, I would force myself to take it anyway. So when I was asked to do the photo shoot, even though it was miles outside my comfort zone, I said yes.

It turns out this would be the first time in my entire twenty-nine years that I wouldn't cringe when I looked at a photo of my body. The photo was taken from behind, of my bare back, and the rolls of flesh on my sides formed a particularly curvaceous hourglass (with a few extra minutes). I found that image, and others from the shoot, more beautiful than I ever could have dreamed, and I proudly shared them on Facebook.

I got plenty of flattering and supportive comments, but I also got nasty ones, including a disparaging remark and a request to remove the images from Facebook because they so offended one "Sarah Lynn." When I clicked on her name, I saw all the telltale signs of an Internet troll. There was no picture or other identifying information, just a sparsely completed profile connected to a handful of friends. "Sarah Lynn," with all of her anonymous bravado, had this to say, verbatim, about my body:

[Note to the readers: the spelling and grammar that follow are "Sarah Lynn's," not my own. Duh.]

Hey nobody wants to see fat rolls!!!!! I would not want my daughter to see this and think its ok to be over weight. Nobody should be proud to be fat they should (you) try to get skinny and show our youth how to loose weight. America is one the most overweight countries in the world and I hate that because fat = lazy.

Her comment was such a perfect, all-encompassing example of the fat-phobia I'd been subjected to for years, and I was so agitated that, in that very moment, I decided I had to respond. And I did—in the form of a makeshift blog titled No Body Shame Campaign.

That was the moment my life changed.

It was responding to "Sarah Lynn" that marked a tectonic shift in the way I viewed myself and how I would choose to live the rest of my life.

In high school a fortune-teller once observed that I had an uncommon "broken lifeline" on my palm. What that meant, she told me, was that I would experience a physical death or possibly a spiritual one, followed by a rebirth. It's something I never forgot (who could?), and looking back, I realize that I was reborn the day I responded to "Sarah Lynn," transformed into a warrior who lived a life of action instead of passivity. That makeshift blog has now been revamped into nobodyshame.com—a worldwide movement that encourages everyone to live their lives free of shame—but it all began with an open letter to my detractor, where I articulated what had taken me nearly thirty years to discover about life and my self-worth.

Here is what I wrote:

Dear "Sarah Lynn,"

I put your name in quotation marks because you're not a real person. I know this because this weekend after I read your comment on a Facebook photo of me (*Damn!! You are a big o' girl*), I clicked on your profile. I quickly realized that your page was a front so that you could say something to me on the Internet that you weren't comfortable putting your real identity behind. But it doesn't matter that you aren't *real*, "Sarah Lynn," because there are a million men and women just like you in the world, and I've officially encountered too many of them to keep my mouth shut about it any longer.

While this is nowhere near the most hateful thing that has been said to me, on the Internet or otherwise, I thought it was a good representation of so much ignorance fat people (and more specifically, fat women) deal with on a daily basis. And since I'm an optimist and you might just really be uninformed and not a hateful asshole, I'd like to address your points.

1. Hey nobody wants to see fat rolls!!!!

Actually, some people do. Some people don't. Some people want to see blond hair. Some people don't. Some people want to see big lips. Some people don't. I would go on, but I reckon this point is pretty elementary and has probably been sufficiently illustrated. Different people like to see different things, and, as human beings functioning in society, sometimes our eyes pass over things we don't find particularly aesthetically pleasing, but we just move on. Because it's easy.

2. I would not want my daughter to see this and think its ok to be over weight.

Unless you plan on keeping your daughter captive in a house full of average or underweight people, devoid of magazines, television, Internet, and other forms of media, she will inevitably see overweight people. She'll see all kinds of people who look nothing like her. She'll see old people, differently abled people, tall people, freckled people, people of all different races . . . and it's certainly "ok" to be all of these people. People are what they are and they can't inherently be "wrong" based on appearance. If you're worried about your daughter becoming overweight, I can assure you that, similar to skin color or stature, being overweight is not contagious. Exposure to my fat body won't cause hers to morph into something it isn't already.

3. Nobody should be proud to be fat . . .

This might shock you, "Sarah Lynn," but I'm not particularly *proud* to be fat. I do happen to enjoy parts of my body—I think I have beautifully shaped breasts and full eyelashes. I like my belly button. I think I have a killer smile. These are all *parts* of my body, but they're not *me*. I am fat. And I am proud of myself. But I'm not *proud of being fat* any more than I'm *proud of being brunette* or *proud of being five-two*. Am I comfortable being photographed in lingerie? Yes. But I wonder if you would look at a woman in a bikini who has size A-cup breasts and say, "Nobody should be proud to have small tits." For some reason, all other women in their various nonfat bodies are just existing—just wearing bathing suits in the summer, tank tops around the house, or lingerie for a boudoir shoot—and no one shames them for that. No one accuses them of having so much *pride* in their bodies that *they aren't afraid to show them.* The implication is that everyone who is not fat is allowed to show their body, but if you're fat and not wearing a potato sack, *Whoa, you'd better check your pride, sister.* I'm proud of myself as an entire person. My body is fat. I deserve to wear the clothes I want and to live the way I see fit just like every other nonfat person. End of story.

4. . . . they should (you) try to get skinny and show our youth how to lose weight.

One of my pet peeves, "Sarah Lynn," is when people assume. I'm sure you're familiar with the old adage about that. I'm almost thirty, and I was not overweight until I was nineteen, so I've actually lived the majority of my little life here on Earth as a "thin" woman, a "normal" woman, an "average" woman, whatever. I've also tried to "get skinny." After being diagnosed with PCOS (save both you and me time and just Google it), I was never able to "get skinny," but I did lose 100 pounds once with the help of a wonderful personal trainer and a shit-ton of dedication and hard work. But really, it's no concern of yours what I *should* do with my body.

5. America is one of the most overweight countries in the world and I hate that because fat = lazy.

I will agree with you there: America is one of the most overweight countries in the world. But I must wholeheartedly disagree with your statement that "fat = lazy." Some fat people are lazy. Some aren't. Some thin people are lazy. Some aren't. Again, it's not any concern of yours if I'm lazy or not, but . . . I'm actually not. And plenty of fat people aren't. I'll never forget the time I busted my 250-pound ass at the gym, outperformed all of the thin people in there, ran four miles, and walked out to the sidewalk dripping with sweat, only to be greeted with "Hey, fat-ass!" from a passing car.

This blog post was the beginning of my new life. It's a life I never could have conjured up even in my wildest imagination—one full of genuine confidence, happiness, and respect for the old life I survived. To call this change in my psyche a "rebirth" isn't the least bit overdramatic, either; I am actually living in a way that I previously thought impossible. Sometimes I still have to pinch myself.

When confronted with all the implausible circumstances, auspicious opportunities, and boundless reserves of love (for myself and others) that have appeared in my life, I often wonder how in the world I got here.

Here's how . . .

2

I WASN'T A FAT KID—BUT I GRADUATED KINDERGARTEN WITH BODY-IMAGE ISSUES

"Oh, honey, that's not chocolate milk." My mother tapped her long red nails against the gallon of chocolate milk at which I was pointing. "That's just white milk in a brown container."

I may have been only five, but I knew that my mother, who was now pushing the grocery cart past the milk—the chocolate milk—and shooting me a backward sympathetic glance, was a liar. She desperately needed an excuse to explain why I couldn't have my favorite drink, when the truth was that my pediatrician had concerns about my weight and had instructed my mother to restrict my chocolate milk and ice cream intake.

In the early mornings, hearing the familiar clacking sound of my mother stirring Nestlé Quik into a tall glass of milk was the overture to every good day. Those days ended with a bowl of chocolate-and-vanilla swirl, which she scooped from the gigantic tub in the freezer. I usually requested that she zap it in the microwave for thirty seconds, and then I'd sit in the kitchen, or

Rocking my bathing suit during the summer before my first diet (1988).

My first soccer game as a Pink Panther (1990).

outside at the patio table if it was warm enough, and savor every spoonful. In between my favorite treats there were lunches of ham sandwiches on white Sunbeam bread (cut into "teepees" for me and "houses" for my brother, Hunter) with a handful of Doritos on the side. For dinner my mom served our family sensible meals like meat loaf with broccoli, always flanked by a tiny side salad and an icy glass of sweet tea.

While adjectives like "skinny," "lanky," or "bony" have never been used to describe me as a child or otherwise, until the is-it-or-isn't-it-chocolate milk showdown in the dairy section of Kroger, I'd never had a second thought about what or how much I ate, much less about the consequence either had on my body. An average American five-year-old in 1989 stood 44.2 inches tall and weighed 44.3 pounds.* According to the old medical records I've dug up in the years since, I stood 45.5 inches tall and weighed 46 pounds. I certainly don't think my extra pound or so qualified me as a porker, but evidently it did for the pediatrician. So, just after preschool, I was indoctrinated into diet culture. It would be more than twenty years before I had any idea what that meant.

I was a precocious child with lopsided bangs, courtesy of my dad's barber, and a never-ending tank of energy and curiosity. I dressed as much like a tomboy as I did a princess, piecing together outfits of Ocean Pacific surf-wear complemented by plastic jewelry and pink jelly shoes that caused my mother to proclaim in her saccharine Southern accent, "Oh, Whi-itney, you're a viii-sion!" I eagerly joined a recreational soccer team and skipped along in an honorary uniform to my dad's softball games where he was the coach, Hunter was the bat boy, and I the ball girl. Hunter was four years older, and we played outside every day. We skinned our knees climbing trees, chased our sweet but unsuspecting Pomeranian around our backyard, rode our bikes in circles around the block, and didn't come home until the sun went down. This was 1990, of course, so there were no iPads or DVR'd episodes of our favorite television shows tempting us to stay indoors. We did have an early-edition Nintendo, but we preferred active games like Duck Hunt and racing each other on the Power Pad.

The piece of technology that really got us going was my dad's enormous, clunky, RCA camcorder, which he used to record Hunter and me re-creating scenes from our favorite movies like *Rambo* (which is undoubtedly why I harbor a crush on Sylvester Stallone to this day—don't judge me). Even though Hunter al-

---

* Ogden CL, Fryar CD, Carroll MD, Flegal KM. "Mean body weight, height, and body mass index, United States 1960-2002." Advance data from vital and health statistics; no. 347. Hyattsville, Maryland: National Center for Health Statistics, 2004.

ways made me play the Russian when we reenacted *Rocky IV*, my brother was nothing short of heroic to me, so I was more than happy to be cast in whatever play, movie, or skit he dreamed up. I took my role of supporting actress very seriously. Hunter was all too quick to remind me that if I messed up or forgot my lines, he could easily replace me with Spencer (the Pomeranian). Much to my embarrassment, we have video evidence of Hunter lip-synching "Fat," Weird Al's parody of Michael Jackson's "Bad" into a toy microphone while I bounce on our mini-trampoline with a basketball stuffed up my shirt, dropping a plastic hamburger bun, patty, and toppings beside my tilted open mouth onto the floor. Dad gets a close-up while I sing off-key, "Shamone!"

Despite my apparent clairvoyance, honing my psychic skills didn't appeal to me. I discovered my true passion in life (no, it's not the chocolate milk, either) when Hunter was cast in a community theatre production of *Pippin*, playing the title character as a young boy, and I treasured the evenings that I caught snippets of rehearsals, tagging along with my mom to drop off or pick up Hunter from the theatre. I was transfixed by the show, and within days I'd memorized all the songs and dance numbers. The Fosse-inspired choreography would set my lifelong love of jazz dance in motion, and the ensemble dancers, slithering and swaying in their skintight leotards and bodysuits, with their teased hair and colorful makeup, made me hog-wild with enthusiasm. I'd been dancing at home since I could walk, just moving however I felt. Hunter wrote a song called "Shakin' Fanny." (The lyrics? "Shakin' fanny, shakin' fanny, shakin' fanny-anny!" Repeat.) I, of course, shook my fanny to the amusement of Mom and Dad, who begged us to perform it whenever they had company over. Hunter sang, and I shook, and the adults shrieked with laughter. But the *Pippin* dances were different; they were carefully rehearsed, perfectly controlled, and timed to music in a way I'd never seen. I was dumbstruck.

Mid-curtsy following my "performance" after Pippin. *Mom put pearls on me since we were at the "thee-ay-ter" (1990).*

The dance number from *Pippin* I most liked to imitate was "Spread a Little Sunshine." The song was performed by a woman named Amie who would eventually become my real-life dance teacher ten years later. I executed all of the sassy moves and hip thrusts with gusto, even though the sexual innuendo was lost on me completely. I took to performing it nightly for my mother and father, who encouraged me to show Amie my personal rendition one night after a show.

I surveyed the nearly empty theatre one night as a few audience members milled about before heading home. The black stage, the brightly painted set pieces, the glittering props that would look gaudy and kitschy anywhere else . . . I drank it all in and was devastated when Hunter told me the set had to be "struck." He explained that the carefully constructed castle would have to be disassembled, the props would be returned to a building downtown, and the set pieces would be repainted black again. The thought of this spellbinding place disappearing distressed me more than it probably should have. My parents took note of this, as well as the fact that I literally could not sit still when I heard music. If I was in the car and they were

*Front and center during parent observation day
at Miss Cindy's (1990).*

blasting oldies on the radio, I was convulsing haphazardly beneath my seatbelt to the rhythms of Motown, hitting my back hard against the navy blue seats of our station wagon. If we were watching TV, I jumped off the couch at every commercial jingle, landing on the carpet, thrashing and stepping to the beat. Although I was athletic and enjoyed any kind of exercise in general, my love of dance was intrinsic. I instinctively understood the nuances of how to move my body to a particular kind of music, because I could *feel* it. The melody of a song was all I needed to detect an electric current vibrating in my bones, and, like a conduit, I had no other choice but to channel it through movement. I am still the same way as an adult—you can often catch me tapping my feet in intricate patterns, punching my arms out of open car windows, or waltzing down a store aisle.

My parents dutifully enrolled me in ballet, tap, jazz, and gymnastics classes at the Cindy Gill School of Dance. I was at my happiest when I was suiting up in my tights and leotard twice a week, and I thrived at Miss Cindy's, where classes were small and full of personal attention. My parents were as supportive as I was excited. Each day I rehearsed the dances I had learned at Miss Cindy's, with my mother repeatedly reminding me that sitting with my legs wide open in second position was not "ladylike." (And even twenty-six years later, my mother still hasn't given up hope that I will learn to be ladylike. At this point, I'm doubtful.)

Because of my natural ability and unnatural enthusiasm, I quickly became Miss Cindy's star student. Three or four times a year Miss Cindy invited parents to observe the progress their children were making. Both my mother and father attended these classes, my dad lugging the briefcase-size box that contained his camcorder every time. Our VHS collection, which my dad meticulously organized, boasted titles like, "Whitney Dancing at Miss Cindy's Sept. 1990," "Whitney Dancing at Beach Cove Resort," and "Whitney Dancing in Backyard," separated by horizontal lines on the spines. He proudly documented every moment of my childhood dance career, including everything from an improvisational shimmy down a hallway to our annual dance recitals each May.

In one home movie, my dad zooms in on my face and asks me, "What did Hunter say you were going to be when you grow up?"

"He said he's supposed to be an actor and I'm supposed to be a singer and a dancer."

"And what do you want to be when you grow up?" he prompts.

I giggle and say, "I want to work at McDonald's."

My early childhood was picture-perfect, complete with a doting set of parents and a playroom full of toys in our middle-class suburban home. I was so psyched to start school that on the first day I leapt off the front porch and boarded the school bus without giving my parents a kiss goodbye. Heartbroken, they jumped in the station wagon and followed, sheepishly appearing in the doorway of my kindergarten classroom faced with a teacher who assured them that they—not I—would be okay. When the school bus dropped me off again that afternoon, my mom noticed that I looked forlorn.

"Did you make any friends?" she asked.

"Katie P., Katie L., Stephanie, Lindsay, Ashley . . ." I rattled the names off. I wasn't recounting actual people; I had just memorized the names off of the lockers.

"Well, then why are you sad?" Mom implored.

"Because," I sniffled. "We don't get homework until second grade!"

I remedied this disappointment by developing a voracious reading habit, one that my parents grounded me from if I misbehaved at home. Naturally, I circumvented this punishment by squirreling away a flashlight underneath my pillow, and after my dad gave me my nightly back scratch, it was just Dr. Seuss and I staying up late into the night like a couple of lawbreakers.

At school, I was a teacher's pet through and through; I was

chosen for student council, placed in the academically gifted program, and named editor of our school newspaper. I was punished only once, and my outrage over the incident has never dwindled. My class had lined up in the cafeteria after lunch in preparation for the walk back to our classroom, when I bent over at the waist to retrieve my pencil from the floor. A male classmate took this opportunity to (literally) kiss my ass and I whipped around upright and slapped him in the face. But when we got back to our classroom, *I* was the one who got punished. I wailed over the injustice for more than an hour and refused my nap time as a form of protest. It seems that, even then, I had all the feisty makings of a feminist.

In fifth grade at Miss Cindy's, I was chosen to dance the lead in our recital piece, based on *The Wizard of Oz*. Since I was Dorothy, I braided my long brown hair into pigtails, wore the blue-and-white checked dress, ruby slippers, and carried a stuffed dog in a picnic basket.

But most important, I got to dance in every dancer's most coveted spot: front and center. And when I was front and center, because of my attention to detail in dance class, I began to observe more than just my own reflection moving in the mirror. I started comparing my body to those of the girls beside me, and I couldn't help but notice that I was larger, both in height and weight, than the rest of my classmates. There was Audrey, who competed in pageants on the weekends. She had long chestnut hair that she refused to pull back, but when she repeatedly whacked me in the face with it, I couldn't even be annoyed; I was too enamored with the grown-up-shampoo smell it had. There was our assistant teacher's niece Brittany, a diminutive wisp of a girl with white-blond curls, who always suspiciously ended up on the front row beside me even though her coordination left a lot to be desired. You could be certain that if we were going right, Brittany was going left. And, of course, I was jealous of my best friend, Nicole, who'd been dancing with me ever since we

*From my fifth-grade dance recital—the same year I earned the
title "Baby Beluga" (1995).*

first started at Miss Cindy's and was in my fifth-grade class at school. I couldn't help wishing I had her thick, curly hair, slight stature, and olive complexion instead of what I deemed my awkward, bottom-heavy figure, lackluster hair, and paler skin.

It didn't matter *who* I was looking at in dance class, because all the girls were smaller than me. They had spaces in between their thighs where I had only flesh; they were as flat as a board from their collarbones to their knees, but my stomach was rounded and my upper thighs protruded with thickness; these girls wore a size small in our dance costumes, but I wore a large. Already five feet tall and weighing 100 pounds, I wasn't skinny, nor was I muscled. Although my body was strong and flexible, it still appeared soft, in stark contrast to my friends in class who were nothing but skin and bones tacked onto petite frames. As if on cue, I'd gotten underarm and pubic hair the year before, immediately after we'd taken the "What's Happening to My Body?" class in school. When my brother noticed, he told me: "Boys don't like girls with armpit hair!"—an assertion I wouldn't challenge until my midtwenties.

It was no surprise to me when Nicole was the first of my friends to start "going out" with some of the boys in our class. I hungered for this rite of passage, too, so I exchanged phone numbers with some of the popular boys and began a ritual of talking to them every day after school. I would take the landline phone from my dad's nightstand, pull the cord out of the doorway and around the corner into my room, and shut the door. I talked about different things with each of them, tailoring the conversation to what interested them the most. One mostly wanted to talk about soccer, while another was more into music. I impressed him with my knowledge of Nirvana, Weezer, Pearl Jam, and Green Day. I relished having access to my brother's cassette tapes, and we'd spend hours listening to music through the phone together, all the while guessing what the lyrics meant. I expected the same friendship, flirtation, and familiarity at school, but I was rebuffed, while they continued to giggle and pass notes with the more popular girls. At recess, when we took to the soccer field, they started mocking me with a song called "Baby Beluga," that ended with, "She's got a whale of a tail!"

My best childhood friend, Nicole, and me (1994).

When that refrain finds its way into my mind these days, it's excruciating to reconcile the fact that they were taunting a 100-pound girl who I would not consider even the slightest bit chubby if I saw a photo of her today. I'd already had my first inklings of self-doubt in the dance studio, and this song proved my negative opinion of my body true. The consensus was that my body was too big. And so the first feeling I ever connected to my body was shame. My body embarrassed me. It caused people to treat me differently in public than they did in private. My body was the kind of thing that inspired schoolboys to sing jeering songs; and it made me feel bad about myself and intensely jealous of others. I started to notice subtle things, like how my soccer shorts bunched up in the middle of my thighs and how they rode up high on my waist if I had my shirt tucked in. I started sitting on the playground equipment during recess, observing instead of participating, afraid of being subjected to that awful song that kept me from feeling happy—and from being who I wanted to be.

Today, this feels a tad melodramatic. All kids are made fun of from time to time, right? It wasn't as though I was an outcast; I still had friends to play with and supportive parents who packed napkins with handwritten notes in my lunch bag and who loved me unconditionally. I was an exemplary student and dancer, and I had the accolades to prove it. But all of this knowledge is tinged with melancholy, because the feelings that burden a young girl when she first becomes conscious of how others view her body don't just disappear one day. They don't fade away when she finally gets a boyfriend or loses five pounds. These insecurities become ingrained in her psyche, piling up like mementos from trips she never wanted to take in the first place and certainly doesn't want to remember.

One night, when I was sleeping over at Nicole's house, we decided to shave our legs for the first time. Afterward, as I sat in front of her mirror, patting tissue against the bloody cuts on my skin, I peered at my reflection. I ran my hand across my face as Nicole stood behind me curling my hair. I picked up a tube of red lipstick and applied it as I'd seen my mother do, smacking my waxy lips together. Later we were being silly, jumping up and down on her bed, and I caught a glimpse of myself in the trifold mirror of her vanity set and thought I was so beautiful.

"If only the boys could see me now!" I squealed as we collapsed in a heap onto the covers. When I stood in front of a mirror, looking only at myself, I could genuinely see my physical beauty. But when I stood in front of the mirrors that lined my dance class, or looked at myself reflected in the eyes of the boys who enjoyed my company but wouldn't go out with me, I felt inferior. They say that comparison is the thief of joy, and this was undeniably true for me. Comparison meant that I couldn't appreciate the fact that *I* thought I was pretty, and by extension, valuable. Because even in fifth grade, I knew that it didn't matter what I thought. It was what my friends thought, what adults thought, and what boys thought, that mattered.

Not long after that sleepover, I saw a TV commercial for an eating disorder clinic. It showed an emaciated woman running on a treadmill, wearing hot pink bike shorts and a shiny blue leotard; the clothes that should have been clinging to her frame hung loosely. Then it cut to a black-and-white shot of a different girl with frizzy brown hair in a baggy sweater slumped against a toilet. The image of the woman with anorexia with her jutting jaw and sunken eyes terrified me, while the bulimic girl looked more or less healthy, if a little sad. And as I lay in bed that night, I prayed to God to make me bulimic, not anorexic. I'm sure I didn't have any realistic concept of what eating disorders were, and I have no explanation for why I thought it was inevitable that I would have one. Or even why I wanted to choose which one would afflict me.

The summer following fifth grade, Nicole and I decided to stop dancing at Miss Cindy's, so when a couple of my friends on our neighborhood swim team suggested that I join, too, I was enthusiastic about learning something new. Even though my swimming skills were limited to the doggie-paddle, I thought it would be fun to be part of the team, and I dove in headfirst. I mastered the basic aspects of freestyle, backstroke, butterfly, and my forte, the breaststroke. When it came time for competition, I was sent to the shark meet, reserved for the second-string swimmers, where multiple swim teams competed against one another at a large community pool. My first event was the fifty-meter breaststroke. Right out of the gate I was the weakest swimmer and the last to slap the tiled wall at the end of the first lap. As I turned and began swimming back toward the diving block, I saw the blurry image of my father, with his signature white hair, standing directly at the end of my lane behind the chain-link fence. As I swam, pumping my legs in the frog position and gasping for air, I knew I didn't want to disappoint him and I didn't want to disappoint myself. I didn't want to come in last. In the final few seconds of the race, I pushed past my closest competitor and finished second to last.

It was a victory my dad and I celebrated after the meet, as we rehashed the event in his classic Jaguar convertible with the top down, me sitting on top of a towel, his favorite oldies compilation CD underscoring the conversation. We shared a cardboard

My first swim meet (1995).

to-go box of cheesy tater tots from Sonic and had one of those life talks that I'll never forget. My dad beamed as he told me how remarkable it was that even in a sport in which I was not naturally talented, I had the drive to better myself and push myself further.

I was proud of myself, but I had mixed feelings about being on the swim team. I loved the water and I loved competing, but I was only happy when I was actually *in* the water. All of the other parts were stressful. When I had to line up for an event without a T-shirt covering my body, I felt naked. My thighs and bum jiggled, and I was sure everyone was staring at me. Sometimes I snuck a T-shirt with me to the diving block, which I would take off only at the very last second to minimize the embarrassment of being seen without one.

I liked hanging out by the pool after early morning swim practice was over, but while many of my friends would change into bikinis and lie out on the lounge chairs that bordered the pool, I never would have dreamed of wearing anything but my sporty TYR suit—a one-piece with thick straps that crisscrossed in the back. I was sure that my parents wouldn't approve of me wearing anything remotely sexy or mature, as I was only eleven, and I also thought those sorts of suits were reserved for girls who had bodies much different than mine. Just like in dance class, I saw exaggerated differences between everyone else's body and mine. Some girls were taller than me by then, and some were more developed, but all were leaner. Then there were the older sisters who also lounged by the pool, their skin darkened by the sun, who never got their hair wet and plopped grown-up magazines over their faces while they worked on their tans. These girls, with their breasts, hips, and painted nails, were fascinating to me, and I spent a lot of time sitting on the edge of my chair, towel wrapped around me as if I'd just emerged from a shower, analyzing their very being.

That summer I got an invitation to a friend's pool party, and so did lots of boys. Lying on my back atop my parents' bed, I discussed the invite with Nicole, twisting the curly phone cord around my fingers while trying to wrap my head around a pool party that had both boys and girls present.

"But I'd have to wear a bathing suit," I told my mother, when she asked if I planned to go to the party. "In front of *boys*." My mother didn't object to my reasoning for not wanting to go, and since she validated my apprehension, I stayed home. Now I can't help but wonder if my mother's own body-image issues caused her to accept my decision without a fight.

At five-four and naturally stick-thin, my mother had been captain of her college synchronized swimming team and had always looked like she sashayed straight out of a magazine. But these days her figure was changing. She had always been a vixen, and I can still picture her in my mind, against the backdrop of our hideous seventies seashell wallpaper, poised in a terry-cloth

The most gorgeous woman in the world:
my mommy (1979).

robe with a turban-wrapped towel on her head, holding a ciga-rette in between her long red fingernails, flicking ashes into an empty Coke can on the bathroom sink. On one unfortunate oc-casion I picked up a Coke can to have a swallow, and instead of delicious carbonated syrup, I got dusty ashes. When I told her in kindergarten (with all the tactlessness one expects from a five-year-old) that her smoking habit embarrassed me, she stopped, cold turkey. In the years after she quit, she'd gained a small amount of weight that filled out her hourglass figure a bit but never caused her to look heavy.

However, five years after she'd quit, she was packing on the pounds in a serious way and, for the first time in her life, found herself significantly overweight. My mother had never revealed how much she weighed, even when she was waiflike, and because she quit posing for photos after her weight gain, I've forgotten how big she actually got. Recently, I was sifting through hun-dreds of family photos when I came across one of my mom, my brother, and me on vacation when I was a preteen. It was rare photographic evidence of my mother at her heaviest, and I was floored at how large she was. She has since lost a ton of weight, more than a hundred pounds, I would guess, and I didn't have this image of my fat, puffy-faced mother in my memory.

"Mom!" I yelled. "Come look at *this*!" She walked into the dining room and saw the piles of photos littering the table. She leaned over to inspect the one I was holding, and stared at me stone-faced.

"Whitney, if you put that in your book, I will never forgive you."

Gaining weight affected my mother deeply. She took to wear-ing stirrup pants and oversize T-shirts and sighed with disgust if she ever caught her reflection. She talked down to herself con-stantly and emphatically refused compliments. A magnet with the words *Fatty, Fatty 2 × 4, Keep Your Hands Off This Door* appeared on our refrigerator. Because of the new stress on her body, she developed aches and pains in her feet and back, so she spent a lot of her time lying on the couch, asking Hunter and me to pick up the phone if it rang. What I can easily recognize now is that my mother was fighting severe clinical depression, but at the time all I knew was that her temper got shorter and things that should have been easy became complicated. She was soon diagnosed with type 2 diabetes and eventually began losing weight, slimming down considerably by the time I graduated high school, and even more after that. She now wears a size 12 or 14, but she still refuses compliments.

Thinking back to that time, and having now experienced clinical depression myself, I have an intense respect for my mother. There are days when I'm *not* depressed that it takes everything in me just to shower and feed my cat. How she managed to fulfill every motherly duty so well while raising two children is beyond my comprehension.

I ended up winning the "Most Improved Swimmer" award that summer, growing two inches and losing about five pounds. I was unaware of the changes until I started sixth grade at my new middle school and a friend gushed at me from several yards down the sidewalk, "You're so skinny!" Being skinny is not my natural body composition, but with the two inches gained and the five pounds lost due to a grueling daily swimming regimen, I had thinned out as much as my body type would allow. The first time I got called skinny was overwhelming. My cheeks flushed, my heart raced, and I glowed as though I'd won some coveted prize.

On my first day of sixth grade I immediately noticed a really cute boy in my homeroom. He had longish dirty-blond hair and wore JNCO jeans. When school was over, my friend approached him, cupping her hands against his ear, asking him if he'd go out with me. He mumbled something back and walked out of the room. As she crossed the classroom, I braced myself for the bad news she was surely about to deliver.

"He said yes," she reported, all matter-of-fact. My mind reeled. "What?" I asked, my voice rising several octaves. "He said yes?" We jumped and clasped hands and raced out of the classroom and down the hallway toward the buses. I was in shock. Since when did cute boys want to go out with me? I bounded onto my school bus, plopping down next to my friend.

"Guess what?" she prompted another friend who was sitting in front of her.

"What?" he asked, half-interested at best.

"Whitney's gonna have a boyfriend."

He raised his eyebrows in surprise. "Haaaa!" he howled, doubling over in his seat and holding his stomach.

"What?" I asked, fearing I already knew the answer.

"No one wants to go out with you," he said firmly. "He's probably playing a joke. You have thunder thighs."

As it turned out, due to some kind of childish sixth grade dating politics that I can't even pretend to remember, the boy in the JNCOs and I ended up not taking the plunge. Still, as the first few weeks of school passed, I realized sixth grade was shaping up to be a far cry from fifth grade. I was actually popular and people weren't making fun of me for being fat. I was suddenly immersed in a new world—one where boys vied for my attention through whispers, phone calls, and love letters, and one where the seat next to me in the cafeteria was never empty.

That autumn we had our first middle school dance. It wasn't a formal event, and I was in my grunge phase, so I arrived at school decked out in my brother's old worn jeans and a flannel shirt, sporting fringe bangs that were appropriate only in the nineties. The dance began directly after class in the darkened gymnasium, and it was phenomenal. Coolio's "Gangsta's Paradise" was blaring and I was gyrating my pelvis within inches of a boy named Paul. Soon, just like in the movies, a circle formed around us, a chain of sweaty preteens chanting, "Go Whitney! Go Pau-al! Go Whitney! Go Pau-al!" After the dance, Paul and I exchanged phone numbers, his written in pencil on the torn edge of his school planner. I talked to him for hours that night, taking my family's new cordless phone into my bedroom closet for supreme privacy. And just like that, Paul became my first boyfriend. Our romance was short-lived, partly because it was sixth grade and partly because he was gay—something I don't think either one of us realized until high school.

With my newfound popularity, I had no trouble finding more boys to take the position of my boyfriend. But that popularity came with a price, I learned. In February, just before Valentine's Day, I opened my locker and a glittery, heart-shaped piece of pink construction paper fluttered out. I smiled inwardly, knowing it must be from one of my admirers. As I bent down to pick it up, I saw my name written on the front in bubble letters, but when I opened it, the message inside was far from sweet. In black Sharpie it read:

> *Die, bitch, die.*
> *From,*
> *Friends.*

I later learned that the culprits were a group of girls whom I considered to be my friends. Soon, the "Baby Beluga" song from fifth grade was replaced with a new one. This one went:

> *Whitney Thore is a whore*
> *On the floor*
> *Of the store*
> *She lies down and asks for more.*

The first time I heard this song about myself, I actually consulted a dictionary, naively searching for the meaning of "whore" in the "H" section. Of course, I couldn't find it. I was twelve years old and, although I'd had boyfriends, I'd never kissed anyone.

By the time sixth grade was over, however, I would have my first kiss and I would also learn the meaning of that word. More important, I would realize that if you were a girl and people didn't like you, the worst thing they could call you was fat, and if you weren't that, calling you a whore was next. (And as a thirty-two--year-old, I hate to report that not much has changed for women.) In some ways I was happy to trade the identity of "fat girl" for "whore." I'm not sure which one I thought was worse. Just like the year before, when I'd seen the commercial for the eating disorders clinic and wished for a mental illness, I was happy to swap being fat for being practically anything else. I'd finally gotten a taste of what it was like to be one of the thin, pretty girls I'd always envied, and I made up my mind that I would sacrifice anything to make sure it stayed that way.

3

I DON'T WANT TO KILL MYSELF
WHEN I LOOK IN THE MIRROR
(ANYMORE)

"When was the last time Whitney saw *90210*?" a girl in the middle school locker room asked, unaware that I could hear her, her voice carrying all the way to where I sat hidden inside a toilet stall.

"I don't know. When?" someone wanted to know. I wanted to know, too, because I'd never seen an episode of *90210*. I clenched, waiting to pee so as not to give myself away.

"When she stepped on the scale!"

A bellow of laughter followed, a raucous noise that sounded more like the entire student body than a handful of girls on the seventh-grade soccer team. I sat frozen until I heard their cleats retreating, tapping toward the rear of the locker room. I exhaled the deep breath I'd been holding, finally peed, and then exited the stall with a dejected sigh. Sixth grade had proven to be like a bratty child who'd bestowed a fantastic toy upon me, only to outstretch its grubby little hands and demand it back the minute I started enjoying it. Just one year had passed since I'd escaped the damnation of being labeled "fat," and I wasn't ready to reclaim the title. As I pumped slimy, Pepto-Bismol-pink soap into my hands, I eyeballed my reflection. In reality, I looked like a completely average seventh grader, neither fat nor skinny, not ugly or striking. But instead of being reassuring, my unexceptional appearance was disheartening. On that day it was like looking into a fun-house mirror that magnified all my flaws and created new ones out of thin air. My brown, shoulder-length hair suddenly seemed mousy and greasy. It wasn't thin, but it wasn't thick enough, either. Unable to decide if it wanted to be curly or stick-straight, it had an annoying wave that never went away. I still had the dreadful fringe bangs that somehow parted in the middle, no matter how many times I tried to wrangle them with my round brush. My face was weird, too, the mirror now confirmed. My natural eyebrows now looked bushy and unmanicured, like caterpillars crawling up my forehead. I had the odd pimple and oily-dry combination skin. The new braces I had weren't helping matters, either. On top of all that, I knew I'd gained a little weight, but I wasn't sure how much.

My popularity with boys was waning, and I hadn't forged many solid friendships with girls, either. My soccer shorts still bunched up in the middle and I stayed awake nights trying to figure out how to rectify it. I'd made the middle school soccer team, which was a small victory, but I was definitely second-string. During our first game I'd stood on the sidelines, preparing to be subbed into the game at any minute. When nearly the whole first half had gone by, I finally took a seat, fielding confused glances from my dad, who didn't understand why my middle school coach wasn't playing me. Two years earlier my dad had begun coaching my extracurricular soccer team when our previous coach quit. Dad didn't know the first thing about soccer, so he checked out library books and videotapes to learn the sport. Through his dedication to coaching, he rose up the ranks, becoming the president of the Greensboro Youth Soccer

Association, and here I was, warming the bench. I wasn't as technically skilled as the girls on the middle school team—they played for the top-tier league outside of school, and I played for the middle tier—but I was an above-average player who always hustled. As my dad instilled in me: "Hard work beats natural talent 99 percent of the time." I tried to remember his words, but it was impossible not to relentlessly compare myself to the other girls. They were skinnier, prettier, faster, and, most important, they were on the field, not the sidelines. They were the ones who joked about my weight when they thought I wasn't around. They were everything I wanted to be. Even now I can still recall the foreboding feeling that came over me when I looked at myself in that mirror hung on the dingy-tiled wall of the locker room. I can feel the pit forming in my stomach that affirmed that I was flawed, and that no amount of hair gel, face wash, or even weight loss could fix entirely. I had been born the wrong way, into the wrong body, and even though I was certain every attempt at correcting this would be in vain, I still had to try. *Hard work beats natural talent 99 percent of the time.*

The day after the *90210* incident, we had sports physicals at school, which meant being weighed and measured in front of everyone. My teammate Anna was in front of me, and I peeked over her perfect shoulder when she got on the scale. She weighed 115 pounds. Then it was my turn. But when the teacher scribbled *117 lbs.* next to my name, I didn't feel relieved. I felt like a fucking whale. My teammate had a nice, slender figure with two pert B-cup breasts and a rounded backside. I wanted to be like her, but I had failed miserably, weighing in a whole two pounds more and standing two inches shorter. I know it seems trivial—two pounds—but to me the difference between my teammate and myself felt like an unbridgeable chasm.

Today, after everything that I've gone through, I want to go back in time and shake those girls on the soccer team and ask them if they had any idea what they were doing—if they had any concept that a 117-pound girl shouldn't be anyone's definition of fat or the butt of a shitty joke. I wish I could go back and shake myself for taking it to heart, and I want to shake my 115-pound teammate, too, because she would later develop full-fledged anorexia and just barely graduate high school.

But my seventh-grade self was rattled by the weigh-in, so when I got home that night, I pulled out a red marker and began writing NL and ND into the daily squares of September, October, November, and December on my soccer-themed calendar. "NL" stood for "no lunch" and "ND" for "no dinner." I'd never eaten breakfast to begin with, and neither did anyone in my family. I figured by cutting my daily calorie intake in half, I could easily reduce my weight. I also began training in earnest outside of school. Four times around my block was roughly a mile, and I began running every day, listening to "Semi-Charmed Life" on my Walkman. (Am I the only one who just realized, like yesterday, that Third Eye Blind was singing about meth, by the way?) My mother begged me to run in the daylight, presumably for safety reasons, but I felt way more secure wrapped in a blanket of shadows, with only the moon poking holes in the darkness.

As the year wore on, I started to notice that the attention I was getting from boys at school became markedly more sexual. Many commented on my "fat ass" and labeled me as "thick." I didn't appreciate either designation, as they both highlighted my fuller figure. When a boy asked me on the phone when he could "hit it," I was oblivious to what he was proposing. Then he asked me when my last period was, and when I told him I hadn't gotten it at all yet, he responded by saying, "Oh man, I wouldn't even have to use a rubber." For a girl who had been kissed only a few times in her life and wasn't even entirely sure what intercourse was, this kind of talk was confusing. I didn't know whether to be grateful for the attention or terrified by it.

By the time spring came, I decided to join the track-and-field

*Posing with my exercise equipment on my thirteenth
birthday (1997).*

team. One day, as I jogged alongside my dad down the street
outside my house, I asked him if running would help flatten my
stomach. He assured me that it would, so I picked up the pace
even more, focusing on the rhythmic sound of my tennis shoes
hitting the pavement while my dad coached me on my breath-
ing. For my birthday in April, I didn't ask for clothes or CDs like
my other friends. Instead, I wanted an Ab Coach, an exercise
mat, and dumbbells, presents I excitedly opened in front of the
fireplace while my dad snapped photos. But I hadn't succeeded
in losing much, if any, weight. I thought back to the commercial
I'd seen two years before and knew it was time to strategically
implement an eating disorder in my life. It seemed like the next
logical step, since modifications to my diet and exercise had
proven fruitless, so I thought the only solution was to do *more*. I
conjured up the images from the commercial that had first

scared me and made me feel uncomfortable and pinned them to a mental bulletin board to use as inspiration and empowerment. Those women, though sick, had willpower, and as far as I could gauge, that was what I needed more of. Besides, I could always stop before *I* got sick.

One afternoon when my parents weren't home, I carried out my plan: I'd already cut down on my food intake, but not so much that anyone had noticed (except my ever-grumbling stomach, that is). I knew that full-blown anorexia would take a commitment to starvation that I wasn't sure I possessed, and I never wanted to look as skeletal and gaunt as the woman I'd seen in the commercial years earlier, so I decided to try my hand at throwing up. I went into my parents' bathroom and wiggled an old toothbrush out of the metal holder attached to the wall, rinsed it off in the sink, and put the handle in my mouth. I inserted it farther and farther down my throat until I felt a tickle and my eyes watered. Still, nothing happened, so I pushed it more forcefully, until I gagged. When the vomit came up, I leaned over the toilet, holding the bar on the shower door to steady myself. When I was done, I flushed and looked in the mirror. Beads of sweat dotted my forehead and my eyes were bloodshot. I rinsed the toothbrush and placed it back in the holder and gargled with my father's Scope.

I was still skipping lunches and dinners, and throwing up became a way to amend mistakes. If I was weak and ate pizza, I could throw up. If I gave in to my persistent hunger pangs and raided the pantry, I could throw up. I grew to crave the hollow feeling of an empty stomach, the red rawness of my throat, and the acidic aftertaste that followed. I felt satisfied, strong, and hopeful. I felt clean.

When I entered eighth grade, I still hadn't lost any weight, and, despite my best efforts, had actually gained. I stood five-two, weighed 125 pounds, and wore a size 6 (sometimes an 8) from the Gap. I shopped at the store 5-7-9—named for the only desirable junior sizes—and I still thought I was enormous. I could not understand how I was gaining weight, considering all the emotional and physical energy I'd poured into getting the opposite outcome. I played soccer, ran track, and continued to compete with the swim team every summer. Now, of course, I know I gained those eight pounds between seventh and eighth grade because I was a young girl going through puberty, but at the time I couldn't fathom why I didn't have control over my body. Regardless, I promised myself that I would never stop striving for perfection. This meant restricting meals, usually skipping lunch, or eating just a cookie from my lunchbox, and throwing up if I ever felt too full. I knew I definitely couldn't stop throwing up; if I had still managed to gain weight while doing it, I didn't want to imagine the consequences of giving it up.

On Halloween, a popular boy named David whom I'd had a crush on since sixth grade invited me and a bunch of our classmates to his house for a party. I attended with two girlfriends who had crushes on two of David's friends. That night, the three boys led us three girls outside, away from the party, to an air-conditioning unit on the side of the house. The A/C hummed loudly as the three boys backed us up against it in a line and began kissing us. Out of the corner of my eye (yes, I was kissing with one eye open, because I was thirteen), I saw Jason's hands fumbling with the waistband of Kristy's jeans, just before I felt David's hands grabbing mine. I didn't feel pressured or uncomfortable in any way, save for the *Oh my God, is this happening?* feeling typical of a teenage girl's first sexual encounter. And then, after a few awkward moments of groping, the three boys all went to third base at the same time. I was excited to hit such a major milestone.

The next week at school, David's two friends and I were talking during social studies class. They were making lewd comments about both of my girlfriends and my heart sank—I knew they had to be saying similar things about me behind my back. I sternly defended my friends and demanded to know how I was any different from them, as we'd all shared the experience together. (Wait, did I just describe a middle school–style orgy? Lord help me.) Whether or not this was my first group sexual encounter remains unclear, but it *was* another one of the first stirrings of feminism I felt. See—contrary to popular belief—unshaven armpits, bra-burning, man-hating, and lesbianism are not requirements for feminism; you just need to commit to sisterhood and to your own voice. (More on that in chapter 10.)

As the end of eighth grade grew closer, I dedicated myself to becoming a better athlete in time for the summer—soccer camp was just around the corner. On days I didn't have practice after school, I went outside with the ball and made myself practice drills until my dad came home. I craved his perpetual guidance. One night he suggested that I try to juggle the ball with my feet. After half an hour I had only managed to make contact with the ball two consecutive times. I went back into the house red-faced and disappointed. But the failure lit a fire inside me, and the next day I returned to my yard determined to be better. I stayed outside until my dad came home and that day I managed to juggle the ball four times, with my dad encouraging me the whole time, reminding me that I could do anything I put my mind to. Months later at soccer camp I won the campwide juggling contest, juggling the ball over a hundred times and beating out just as many girls for the prize.

Instances like this bolstered my belief that maybe anything *was* possible, no achievement was out of reach, and that just because something didn't come naturally didn't mean I would never succeed at it. It simply took hard work, discipline, and willpower. This was the same logic I applied when I set out to change the natural structure of my body, and it frustrated me when I didn't achieve the same results. What I know now that I didn't then is that our bodies are tools we use to develop, strengthen, and hone certain skills, but our bodies themselves have boundaries. Having a certain type of body isn't necessarily something you can acquire; it's genetics.

Frustrated with my inability to control my weight, I began seeking out other things that I could control. I became obsessed with picking at my skin and hair. Every day after school I would run to my mother's bathroom upstairs and begin a squeezing and picking ritual on my face that left my skin blotchy, sometimes bleeding, and covered with fingernail indentations. Then I would pull hairs out of my head. There were specific ones that were darker and coarser than the rest, usually with a stiffer texture. I pulled these out one after the other until I couldn't find any more. When they began to grow back in, I took the tweezers and plucked them out at the root. I got immense satisfaction from this, and soon had a bald spot in the center of my head, right where my bangs met the rest of my hair. My mother, worried about this new development, took me to a dermatologist. I played dumb, too embarrassed to admit I'd been pulling my own hair out. The dermatologist diagnosed me with stress-related hair loss. Well, that's one way to look at it, I thought. I wouldn't learn about trichotillomania, a disorder that causes people to pull out their hair, until high school. But once I got there, it would be the least of my worries.

I was eager to start high school, because just like sixth grade, I thought it offered me an opportunity to start over and to be a different person, to present a shiny new version of myself. When I didn't magically lose twenty pounds or gain the reputation of being one of the popular girls in school, I sought refuge in one of my teachers, a middle-aged overweight woman with a heart of gold. Sometimes we wrote notes back and forth and I told her about all the things that were bothering me, from teenage dramas to my budding bulimia. She urged me to go to the counseling department and confided in me that her sister had been fighting a lifelong battle with bulimia and binge eating. Part of me was shocked to think about an adult still being a slave to such problems, but I didn't see myself becoming one of them. While I appreciated her concern, advice, and sense of kinship, I now wonder at what point an adult should intervene in a child's life and contact her parents—and how my life might have turned out differently if she had.

If my high school was the set of *Clueless,* I wasn't as bumbling and homely as Tai, but I had no hope of being Cher, either. I'd mostly sworn off wearing shorts in order to hide my squishy legs. My wardrobe consisted of jeans and T-shirts. No heels, no skirts (certainly no miniskirts), no spaghetti-strap tank tops. I finally decided to grow out my fringe bangs but didn't wear makeup or style my hair. Halfway through the school year, my mother took me to the spa at the local shopping center and I got my eyebrows waxed for the first time. I felt so chic.

If that was my first rite of passage into womanhood, the second came one freezing January evening on the street outside my house. I sprinted the hundred-yard dash between orange cones my father and I had set up. I ran one after the other, then told my father I had to go to the bathroom. I hurried inside and, to my surprise, just shy of my fifteenth birthday, I got my period. I told my mother, changed my underwear, added a thick, horrible maxi pad, and returned outside to the biting winter air. Junior varsity soccer tryouts were just a month away.

The day before tryouts, I woke up with a scratchy throat, and by late morning my throat hurt so badly that I was unable to talk. My father came to school to sign me out of class. The nurse asked me when my last menstrual cycle was, and I told her it had been four weeks ago. My dad took me home and later asked my mother why she hadn't told him about my period—he felt as though he'd been left out of a significant moment. But at nearly fifteen, I was the only person I knew who'd not yet had her period, and it had long lost its appeal for me. The rest of the day my symptoms became dramatically worse—so much so that I could barely swallow and developed severe congestion in my chest. I was going to miss soccer tryouts and I was devastated. My father called the coach, who said there would be a makeup tryout the next week that I could attend. My illness got worse every day. I went to the doctor, who ruled out strep throat and the flu. I lay around the house, coughing up phlegm and drooling into a washcloth because my raw throat couldn't handle swallowing my own saliva. One morning, I was coughing and hacking when I spit up a piece of black matter. I called my dad to look at it. He assured me it was nothing and that it happened to him "all the time." When he tucked me back into his bed and went downstairs to leave for work, I heard him on the phone with the doctor.

"Yes, it's black. I've never seen anything like it. Is that normal?" We never did figure out what it was.

On the fourth day or so of my sickness, I started bleeding again, right on schedule. But this period was different than the first. I was bleeding through a pad every hour, my stomach was cramping, my back was aching, and I could feel blood oozing out of me every time I coughed. It was not only the heaviest period I would ever have, but the last nonmedically induced one I would have for the next seven years. It finally ended a week later and I returned to school, looking almost gaunt, having lost ten pounds because I was unable to stomach anything during my illness.

"Damn, where'd you go?" a guy friend of mine teased me after class. "Don't go losing that butt now." Even though a few days before I had worried that I was on my death bed, this comment made me flush with pride. Of course it's seventeen kinds of fucked up that weight loss is celebrated even as a result of illness, but I didn't understand that as I walked down the hallways of my high school with a new swing in my step.

Soon after, I saw a flyer posted for the spring musical, *Jesus Christ Superstar*. Even though I couldn't carry a tune, I noted there was a dance audition and thought I'd give it a shot. Showing up to that audition changed the course of my life. It was there that I met Amie again, the same woman whose dances I had imitated during *Pippin* rehearsals when I was five. She cast me as one of six dancers and we launched into rehearsals. I immediately felt motivated, talented, and at home with dancing again. I'd taken three years off from dance classes, but now, after the first fifteen minutes of learning choreography, I felt more inspired than I had ever felt before. The whole process of *Jesus Christ Superstar* was rewarding, from rehearsals, to forging a relationship with a new dance teacher, to the teamwork involved, to the high of performing and the praise I received—it was all-consuming. I was, once again, hooked on dance.

Since Amie also taught dance at Weaver Center, a special performing arts school in my town that offered advanced dance and theatre classes that public school students could take within their regular school day, I made it my goal to gain admission there. I had the passion, the drive, the natural talent, and the basic skills that I had acquired in childhood, but when it came to the more technical elements of leaps and turns, I was miles behind. I attended an audition at Weaver Center one spring night near the end of the school year. I had gone to the local dancewear store and purchased new leotards, dance pants, leg warmers, and shoes. But in the audition, even though I looked like a dancer, I failed to perform like one. The dance combination was more modern than anything I'd done before, and the instructor taught it without any counts. I was stuck in the back with a bad view, feeling—and looking—completely lost. I was mortified.

After the audition was finished, I walked out to my mom's car through the rain with my eyes turned downward on the puddles underneath my feet. When I explained to her that I'd never danced worse in my life, she didn't try to convince me otherwise. My parents raised me to be self-aware, and while they showered me with positive reinforcement for a job well done, they never tried to convince me that I was better at something than I thought I was in an effort to spare my feelings. A few days later I learned that I was placed in the Honors Advanced Dance class after all. In hindsight, it shouldn't have surprised me so much. Amie likely paid less attention to my one-minute audition and more to the months I worked with her during *Jesus Christ Superstar*. Just recently, on one of my dance videos on Facebook, she commented:

> Who wouldn't love a fifteen-year-old choreographer, dedicated performer, peer motivator, etc. You were easy to teach and love. Amazing then and now.

Amie was the first of three women who shaped my dance career. I would meet the second just two months later, when I auditioned for a community theatre production of *Carousel*. I hadn't had much luck as an actress, unlike my brother. He'd been cast in several community theatre productions as a child, and was a member of the prestigious theatre company at Weaver. Now he was performing at Appalachian State University where he was pursuing a degree in theatre performance. However, when I saw the flyer for *Carousel*, a dance-intensive summer musical, I thought I might have a chance. Since I'd loved *Superstar* so much, I decided to give it a shot. During the music portion of auditions I gritted my teeth and struggled through a few bars of a song and scales alongside the piano. Then I changed into shorts, a T-shirt, and my worn Adidas Gazelles for the dance portion of the audition. This is where I met my second dance master, Marie.

Marie was a riveting, take-no-shit kind of woman and she captivated me. While she called out counts and demonstrated the movements, most of the other people auditioning—who were not dancers—exchanged terrified glances and nervous giggles as Marie quickly moved from one element to the next. The routine ended with us going down to the floor in a way that would have caused a nondancer to vomit, but it didn't faze me.

A few days later I made the familiar trek from the parking lot to the City Arts building, steeling myself against the probable rejection. When I got to the glass window where the cast list was posted, I could hardly believe it when I found my name listed under the ensemble dancers. Once rehearsals started, Marie immediately took a liking to me because I worked harder than anyone else. I memorized choreography after she taught it once. I rehearsed it on my own time. I made corrections the first time she pointed them out. One day in rehearsal she roared, "Is Whitney the only person who heard me when I told you to kick out your foot when you get to the end of the steps?"

Marie intrigued me with her raspy voice, her T-shirts with the necks cut out that she wore with combat boots, and the way she stood smoking cigarettes. But mostly I admired her self-assuredness. She was tiny, with light blue eyes, curly dark blond hair, and a riotous laugh. She was thirty and so . . . cool. A graduate of UNCG—the University of North Carolina at Greensboro—she was now part of the Jan Van Dyke dance company, an avant-garde group that appealed to my thriving artistic senses. She taught classes in the cultural arts center during the day, charging seven dollars per person. It was in these classes that I truly became a dancer. Her choreography was way out of my reach, but I pushed and struggled through each class, dreaming about the studio from the time one class ended to the time the next one began. I will never forget the first time, during dance class, that Marie called out, "Good girl, Whitney!" It was an honor like none other.

Before one of her classes, I'd been talking with a male fellow dancer about how I wanted to lose twenty pounds. I weighed 120 at that point, and I fervently subscribed to the belief that I was supposed to weigh 100 pounds at five feet, and an additional five pounds for each inch. At five-two, that meant I should weigh no more than 110 pounds. Naturally, I thought I'd overachieve and go for 100. My friend blurted out to Marie, "Whitney wants to lose twenty pounds. Isn't she crazy?"

Marie turned toward us abruptly and snapped, "Whitney, if you lose twenty pounds, I won't let you take my class." And with that the discussion was over. Obviously, Marie didn't understand my need to lose weight, probably because she was thin herself, I reasoned. I disregarded her admonishment and narrowed my eyes at my friend.

As it turns out, Marie understood more about the perceived need to lose weight and its effects on young girls'—specifically dancers'—self-esteem than almost anyone. I spoke with her in the beginning of 2016 (for the first time in over a decade), after she'd seen a YouTube video I posted and she sent me this message:

> I just gotta say . . . guurrlll . . . you are one bad-ass bitch (and I mean bitch in the best way possible, it's a compliment coming from me—I, after all, am one, so I don't throw that term around lightly—it's a title that has to be earned . . .). Negative body image is a real thing and one that as a dance teacher I deal with all day every day. What you are doing with your show and your social media posts is invaluable, and at the risk of coming across as patronizing, I am so proud of you and so proud to be able to count you as one of my former students. Keep up the good work, lady . . .

My sophomore year was filled with firsts, and most of them weren't positive. I got my first C, in geometry, and I smoked my first cigarette. I was plagued by moodiness and I started fighting a lot with my mom. But finally in the spring, for the first time that year, I began to feel excited about my future again. I had been cast as Cha-Cha in *Grease,* my parents were going to Europe for two weeks, and my brother Hunter (who would already be finished with his college courses) would be staying with me. Plus, I would be studying drama at Governor's School, an elite summer program held on a college campus, which I'd been admitted to after auditioning. Even though my morose nature was beginning to transition into depression, I clung to this timeline of events, willing myself to be content with it, but my constant battle with my bulimia, body image, and self-esteem lingered, in no small part due to feedback from my peers.

There was a boy named Nick in my humanities class who often flirted with me. One day in class he tapped me on the shoulder, announcing an observation that people seemed all too happy to share with me.

"My brother says you're fat."

Grease went off without a hitch, and when my parents left for Europe, my twenty-year-old brother gave me one rule: go to school. But I didn't always abide by it. I once skipped an entire day with an older girlfriend, listening to music and smoking weed for the first time, in some guy's filthy apartment. My brother decided to have a party on the same night as the prom, and, aside from being literally the only party I ever went to in high school, it was the biggest party of the year. A couple hours before anyone got to our house, I drank my first beers and got high with my friends. By the time my-brother-says-you're-fat Nick showed up, I was drunk and completely unaffected by his presence.

The next morning Nick shyly handed me a folded-up piece of paper. In it was a desperate plea for me to forgive him for calling me fat. He was headed to college in the fall and wrote that he couldn't bear to leave without knowing where things could go with me. I still have that folded-up piece of paper because I'm overly sentimental, but I called Nick and told him any mutual liking we had for each other was over. Not only had his declaration of his brother's opinion of me hurt me deeply, but in order to get past it, we'd have to discuss it, and that meant talking about me being fat, which was more demoralizing at the time than anything I could imagine.

I arrived at Governor's School a few weeks later, about an hour and a half away from my home. The first thing I noticed about my roommate was the way her clavicle protruded like a built-in necklace of bone beneath her white halter top. She had tanned skin and thick, straight hair. The feelings of inferiority that I'd hoped to leave at home were still following me like a faithful friend.

Governor's School was structured a lot like college: while most of your time was spent in a specialized area, we had other classes with all kinds of students. During the first break on our first day, some girls were lined up on the quad, lying out in bikini tops and microscopic, cutoff jean shorts. I lay there, too, on my stomach at the far end of the line. I didn't even own a bikini and certainly would never have worn it in a public setting like that, so I just lounged in my overalls and T-shirt. I watched as a group of guys approached us. Starting at the end opposite me, they chatted or made a joke with each bikini-clad girl. When they got to me, they just walked right on past without acknowledging my existence at all. The obvious snub was another wake-up call: this summer would not go as planned. In fact, it would be the backdrop to my darkest days.

My room was a common place for a bunch of the girls on the

hall to gather, and we gossiped about boys and told one another about our lives at home. One night, a girl pointed to the stack of VHS tapes next to the TV and asked what they were. When I told her they were videos of my old dance performances, several of the girls coaxed me to pop one in the VCR, so I did. The videos weren't great quality, and one of the girls burst into laughter as she watched the grainy moving images on the screen.

"Who's that fat one?" she demanded to know, gesturing toward the TV. "She sucks." She was talking about me.

The group stayed up late and eventually the topic of conversation turned to weight loss. One girl was a gymnast and her eyes lit up as she recounted how she lost weight.

"I eat anything I want in the morning. Seriously. Bagels, doughnuts, bacon, whatever. But then I don't eat the rest of the day, and I just started dropping weight." It was an approach I had never considered, and I wrote it down in one of my notebooks so I could try it out later.

Another night, we were all hungry, so we ordered a pizza and walked to the nearest shopping center to load up on ice cream and junk food. Even though our room had a minifridge, mine was always empty, because unlike many of the other girls, my parents hadn't stocked it with snacks. Once, on the phone with my dad, I complained about this, most likely in a bratty way, and he retorted, "You don't need to be eating anything extra!"

We all binged that night, stuffing our faces until we couldn't manage another bite. We took a silly photo, holding up our boxes of ice cream while we linked arms and brought the spoons to our lips. Afterward we each purged in the hall bathroom, one after another with the door open, congratulating one another on a job well done. This particular memory disturbs me more than almost any other, not necessarily because of the bingeing and purging, but because of the collective nature of it. Sure, it was something we'd all done—but privately, away from the eyes and judgments of others. It was a secret we all scrambled to keep. Why did we think it was something so benign, so common, so *normal,* that we were willing to do it together with the same ease with which we went shopping or painted our nails?

I soon got hit with the biggest bout of depression I've ever experienced in my life. I've spent many years in varying states of depression since, but I've never endured anything so bleak. To this day, sixteen years later, when I recall how despondent and how hopeless I felt, it terrifies me. And any time I feel the black cloud descending again, I'm paralyzed with the fear that it will consume me like it did then.

The source of my depression was, I'm certain now, clinical. It would be an awful injustice to chalk it up to simply not feeling like I fit in with my peers. In my philosophy class, we spent entire periods tackling existential questions, the kind that made your mind spin and didn't have answers at all. Not having answers bothered me, and those abstract, answerless questions plagued me and made me incredibly anxious. While my classmates raced toward the cafeteria or horsed around outside, I spent a lot of time curled up in a ball on my bed, listening to Tori Amos on my Walkman, burrowing deeper into depression. I wondered what would happen when I died, and what would happen after that. I didn't want to exist forever, in heaven, or in the cosmos, or anywhere, for that matter. I had an overwhelming appetite for nothingness, where I wouldn't have to feel any pain. On top of that, I felt like the work we were doing in theatre class was phony. We were doing a performance based on Plato's Allegory of the Cave, which I loved, but the performance itself seemed like nothing more than artificial performance art. While my classmates cried and waxed poetic about how meaningful it was, I thought it was contrived. And I thought they were stupid.

One evening I was sitting alone by a fountain when a boy

named Derek struck up a conversation with me. He had dark auburn hair, subtle freckles, a killer smile, and was chubby in the way dudes are allowed to be. Like most students there, he was a year older than me, and as it turned out, he lived in Greensboro, too, but attended a different high school than I did. We hung out for a couple hours, laughing and flirting. When the sky started to look like cotton candy, he leaned over to kiss me. He asked me to go to a dance with him a couple nights later and I enthusiastically agreed. I was smitten.

I was puzzled when Derek was a no-show on the night of the dance. I walked around the gymnasium at least three times, cutting through clusters of sweaty bodies to look for him. Hours later I finally spotted him passing me on the quad with several other guys. He didn't even look my way. He was drunk.

"What the hell?" I said, intercepting him. "I waited for you."

"Whitney, I like you," he slurred inches away from me, his stale-beer breath on my face. "But when I told my friends I was going to the dance with you, they asked me why I would hang out with you when there are so many hot girls here."

By the time his asshole friends had quit snickering and I was able to formulate a reply, Derek was already walking away. I stood there with my entire body prickling as if it were on fire, watching his silhouette shrink smaller and smaller in the distance. I bolted across campus—running away from where Derek's words had pierced me, away from the unbearable truth that I was irreparably damaged, and as far away as I could from other people who could hurt me. When I let myself in my dorm room, I was keyed up and restless and I began pacing the floor back and forth. I felt like insanity was tugging at the edges of my brain. I wanted to get out of this place and I wanted to get out of my body. But that was exactly the problem: I didn't have one defective limb that I could just chop off and be done with it; the problem was my *entire body* and I had no feasible way to amputate the pain. When I finally calmed down, I lay in bed and thought about ways I could kill myself, but I kept colliding with the realization that even death wasn't the end. It didn't matter what I did, where I went, or who I met. The common denominator was me, and I couldn't figure out how to disconnect from my own being. I was doomed to be with myself forever.

4

"FAT" GIRLS HAVE EATING
DISORDERS, TOO

I was eager to leave Governor's School, a place that I could associate only with trite theatrical performances, suffocating existentialism, and painful reminders of my own inferiority. When I returned home I finally got my driver's license, which proved to be a redeeming distraction for a confused and pensive sixteen-year-old girl.

Marie was holding a dance camp at a local university, and I drove to it religiously, seeking refuge inside the dance studio with its mirror that reflected a familiar and comforting image of a dancer who was both talented and respected, even if she was bigger than all the rest.

Each morning, I arrived hungry (literally and figuratively), ready for the hours of challenges and achievements that learning new choreography would bring. It was inside these four walls that I first met Todd, who I quickly appointed my Eternal Dance Partner. He would add Honorary Fat Girl to that title thirteen years later when he joined me in the Fat Girl Dancing video that would eventually amass more than 8.5 million views on YouTube. But at that time, on the heels of such a disap-

At my high school heaviest, the day I got my license—my dad made me wear tennis shoes for the test (2000).

pointing summer, I never could have guessed what our future held.

When Marie announced at the end of dance camp that she would be moving to Los Angeles, I was crushed. Her inevitable absence in my life threatened to extinguish the only fire I had left burning. Marie recruited a bunch of us to help her pack up her things, and I showed up at her house half miserable because she was leaving and half intrigued at being allowed in her personal space. She divvied up tasks among us, assigning me to her bathroom. I examined each cosmetic, hair tie, and bottle of over-the-counter medication closely, handling each one with the utmost care, as if they were mysterious and precious artifacts. I wiped them all clean with a damp cloth and divided them into like items, organizing them into labeled Ziploc bags. At the last minute, I pulled a tube of lipstick out and leaned over the sink into the mirror. Glancing at the open door, I painted my lips quickly with it and dropped the tube back in the bag. When I was done, Marie stood next to me investigating my work. I began explaining the specifics of my packing system, but she interrupted me.

"Thank you. I knew you'd do it perfectly."

Before we left, a classmate of mine implored me to eat a slice of the pizza Marie had bought us as a thank-you, but I declined. Catching the conversation from the porch, Marie barked at him.

"Leave her alone," she said. "If she doesn't want it, she doesn't want it."

When I drove away from her house that day, I ran my tongue over my lips so I could taste Marie's lipstick, thinking about what my life would be like without her. A few weeks later when my junior year of high school began, I was the heaviest I'd ever been, weighing more than 150 pounds. My dad, who was well aware of my dissatisfaction with my weight, suggested I see a nutritionist. I was in complete agreement and was hopeful that this would be the thing to finally help me shed some pounds and gain everything I lacked. My dad found a nutritionist and gave me directions to her office, just a few minutes from our house. When I parked, a tingle of excitement shot up my spine, and I started up the steep, carpeted staircase to her office.

The nutritionist's name was Beverly. She was middle-aged and elegant, with a dark gray bob and a kind voice. During the initial consultation she asked me about my eating habits. I explained to her that I didn't eat breakfast and sometimes skipped lunch, but usually ate dinner. I never ate fast food, but I enjoyed smoothies and carbs; sandwiches and pasta were my favorite things to order in restaurants. I tentatively told her about my past with purging, not even sure whether I had a full-blown eating disorder. She asked me why I wanted to lose weight, and I told her that I wanted to be a better dancer and athlete, and that I felt pressure from both my father and, well, the world, to be thinner. At the mention of my father, Beverly lowered her eyes and said, "When he called me . . . he said something. And I told him never to repeat it in front of you again." To this day I have no idea what she was so ominously referring to, but I can only guess it was the kind of careless remark that my dad considered to be well-meaning but Beverly recognized as damaging, like his admonishment of "you don't need to be eating anything extra!" just a couple months before.

After she'd assessed my habits and motivation for weight loss, she went over the basics with me: a sensible portion of anything should be no bigger than my fist, eight glasses of water a day was a necessity, and high protein was key. She spread out a collection of labels she'd removed from store-bought food and flat boxes empty of their previous contents. She showed me how to read the nutritional information and pointed out the serving sizes. She compared different brands of protein bars and championed beans, vegetables, and plain whole-grain cereals, while warning me about the sugar content in the smoothies I liked so much. Then she pulled out a premade calendar and a handful of pens and highlighters, and we began meal planning. We decided on easy breakfasts, like a hard-boiled egg, lunches of turkey sandwiches and a piece of fruit, and dinners of grilled chicken and broccoli.

When I left her office that day and returned home, I was determined to follow the plan perfectly, and I did. I forced myself to eat breakfast, even though I much preferred feeling concave until midafternoon. I ran home for lunch to scarf down a quick sandwich my mother had prepared. I chugged liters of diet, fruit-flavored water all day, which caused me to urinate incessantly. At the end of my first week following Beverly's diet plan, I returned to her office and hopped on the scale, salivating in anticipation of what it would show. I had lost *seven* entire pounds and I felt amazing, even a little smug, about my progress. At home, my parents met me with high-fives and spirited congratulations, but my success came to a quick stop not even one week later. During week two I followed the plan exactly the way I had the week before, with purposefulness and precision, but when I weighed in at Beverly's office, the scale said I had gained three pounds, making a liar and a fool out of me. How is this possible? I wondered silently, my cheeks burning with the embarrassment of failure.

Beverly had found my gain curious, but urged me not to let it derail the process. Too late. In just fourteen days I had become completely disenchanted with dieting "the right way." I wanted weight loss to be a simple equation. If I ate x and y, and knew the value of each, I should be able to figure out the answer, every single time. But it was obvious that losing weight would not be so easy, and right then and there I decided to abandon Beverly's highlighted meal plans full of chicken and beans and take control of the situation myself. Even though I kept seeing Beverly, I filled out her meal plans with lies, jotting down a hard-boiled egg here or a protein bar there that never touched my lips.

Despite my ongoing weight loss frustrations, I was determined to be more optimistic about this school year than I had been in years past. For starters, I was one of four juniors who had been accepted into the Ensemble Theatre Company at Weaver Center, so now I had dance class there in the morning, a few periods at my regular high school, followed by a return to Weaver for my two-hour theatre class. It was in my early morning dance class that I first met Leslie, the third woman who would shape my dance career. Leslie had just joined the team at Weaver, and after she observed my class one morning, she approached me and asked if I took dance anywhere else locally.

I told her I had not danced in an extracurricular setting since I left Miss Cindy's after fifth grade, and she invited me to her studio that afternoon to take a class with her senior competition company, which was composed of her most talented dancers. I was thrilled at the invitation and apprehensive about what it would entail.

When I entered Greensboro Dance Theatre later that day, I was greeted with the familiar sound of tap shoes clacking as younger students filed out of the studio in front of me. The black marley felt smooth underneath my bare feet as I tossed my bag in the corner, and, as usual, when we lined up at the barre to begin a ballet warm-up, I was noticeably heavier than the rest of the girls in the class. I was sandwiched in between two tall, long-necked, slender dancers, and we started in first position and began moving our feet in time to the predictable sound of classical piano. Even on my best days I had never been adept in ballet, and as we moved on to tendus, dégagés, and battements, I struggled to keep up with the pace. By the time we began our floor work, crossing the room from corner to corner in a combination of tombé, pas de bourrée, glissade, and jeté, I felt completely out of my element.

The atmosphere of Leslie's studio was different from the musical theatre rehearsals and classes I'd been attending at Weaver. There, the emphasis had been on choreography, expression, and performance; at Greensboro Dance Theatre, the emphasis was on technique. Leslie had a dress code (a specific leotard and tights), which left me feeling exposed and fatter than ever, not to mention that her dancers took instruction much more seriously, which made it painfully obvious I hadn't danced in a class setting like this for the last five years. Still, even though my thick thighs and lack of technique threatened to shake my identity as a dancer, I took it on as another challenge, and in a few months I was dancing on pointe (albeit wobbly and poorly) and teaching a hip-hop class for children and adults.

Teaching this class was my first paid job, and I took my title of Dance Teacher seriously. Most of the students who signed up for my hip-hop classes had never danced a day in their lives, and I delighted in introducing them to the concept of moving their bodies for pleasure. Because they were less experienced, they were simultaneously more uneasy and more fearless than some of my own classmates. They approached instruction with trepidation initially, but once they built their confidence even the slightest bit, they were enthusiastic and insatiable learners. I was amazed by their wide-eyed trust in me and eagerness to accomplish more than they ever thought possible. The earnestness of my students was inspiring. I quickly realized that I not only loved teaching, but I also had a knack for it.

Conventional wisdom would tell you that with the addition of Leslie's twice-weekly, two-hour dance classes and teaching the hip-hop classes on top of everything I was doing physically (one hour of dance at Weaver daily, twice-weekly ninety-minute soccer practice, and weekends full of soccer games and dance competitions and conventions), I would have been able to drop a few pounds without even trying, but this was not the case. I still weighed myself daily, as some kind of torture, and my dad always asked for the result. One day in particular, as I was rushing out of the house for school, I told him I hadn't lost any weight the previous day.

"Well, what did you eat yesterday?"

"A sandwich," I told him.

"Well, tomorrow," he suggested, "don't eat the sandwich."

I know now how awful this sounds, but my dad was—and sometimes still is—incredibly misguided about weight loss, like so many of us are. He is remarkable and result-driven in all areas of his life. In his mind, he was proposing a way to get the results I wanted and nothing more. He wasn't thinking about the fragile self-esteem or distorted body image of a teenage girl. After all, it was the same way he had approached his own weight loss over the years. I can't count how many times he has told me about severely restricting his food intake for a few days in order to shrink his stomach to make consuming less food easier.

I was still seeing Beverly and trying to eat as little as possible when I became reacquainted with a guy named Shawn while doing a local community theatre production in the fall. I'd met Shawn the year before, when he was running crew for the community theatre production I was involved in. (I'd also met Tal and Buddy then, who are two of my best friends to this day.) We'd dated briefly and hastily broken up at my school's Sadie Hawkins dance, which we called TWIRP—an acronym for The Woman Is Required to Pay. It was a short-lived romance and I think we kissed maybe twice. However, when I met him again in the same theatre a year later, things were different—armed with a license, my first pair of high-heeled boots, and an air of sophistication only junior year could bring, I found myself interested in him again and my hormones were raging. We decided to give dating another go, and before I could blink, we fell madly in love with each other in the way that only high school virgins can.

Shawn was strong, stocky, and intoxicatingly handsome. He played football at a neighboring high school but had none of the stereotypical negative trappings of a high school athlete. He was romantic, sensitive, and thoughtful. He wrote me poetry, made me Tori Amos CD compilations, and snuck packs of cigarettes into my car. Best of all, he was wholly and completely enamored with me, and I with him.

Shawn was highly intelligent and an integral part of his school's Science Olympiad program—he had all the makings of a budding engineer (which he would later become). With his average GPA and penchant for getting detention due to missed homework, he was just enough of a "bad boy" to appeal to me.

In the bathroom at one of his football games, an acquaintance offered me an Adderall pill, telling me to split it in half. I had only smoked weed twice and gotten drunk once (both times when my parents were out of town). I had a strict ten-thirty curfew, and I certainly didn't "party," so most drugs were completely off my radar. I won the D.A.R.E. essay contest in fifth grade (I told y'all I was a model student), and the thought of mind-altering substances generally scared the shit out of me. But because I viewed this as a medication and my friend said it would curb my appetite, anxiety, and depression, I decided to give it a try.

One half-pill of Adderall exhilarated me. Suddenly, life exploded in Technicolor, and any inklings of sadness and depression were erased by the tingling, dry-mouthed euphoria that the pill brought on. I immediately asked for more. When I was on Adderall, I was happier and more motivated than ever; I could listen to my teachers in class and take notes while simultaneously editing a classmate's paper. Each moment thrummed with creative energy. Even a few minutes at a stoplight could turn into an impromptu choreography session in my car. I became exuberant, my handwriting improved dramatically, and my appetite completely evaporated. The last of these side effects was the most rewarding, of course, and restricting my food became effortless. I subsisted on soda and coffee, taking one to two Adderall pills every morning. One day, I rushed in the house as usual for lunch and dismissed the pimento cheese sandwich my mom offered to me. I had been throwing them out for weeks and finally started refusing them altogether. As I grabbed a Coke from the fridge and flew out the back door, my mom called after me, begging me to take the sandwich.

"I'm fine, Mommy!" I yelled back, to which she cocked her hip and asked me jokingly, "Whitney, are you on drugs?" It wasn't until a few weeks later when a student approached me in the parking lot at school, telling me he'd heard I had Adderall and asking me if I had any to sell, that I realized I actually was.

Of course, my favorite side effect of Adderall (appetite suppression) didn't last twenty-four hours a day, and I didn't like eating at home under the watchful eye of my parents, so Shawn's house became a safe haven for me. His mom stuffed the fridge with lunch meats and there were always chips and cookies in the pantry. When I was really hungry, I would make two bologna sandwiches, each with two pieces of white bread, mayonnaise, mustard, and a slice of American cheese, and then I'd throw a couple handfuls of chips on my plate. After eating this kind of meal, I would retreat to the only bathroom in their one-story home and turn on the water to mask the sound of my vomiting. Shawn was aware of this habit, as I also purged each time we went out to our favorite restaurant for dinner, where we would drink sweet tea and chain-smoke while I waited for my regular meal of fettuccine Alfredo and broccoli. Sometimes I'd order apple cobbler for dessert, but I always went to the bathroom to get rid of it as soon as the last bite hit my stomach. Shawn in no way approved of this routine and told me so every time I returned from the bathroom with bleary eyes and smeared makeup.

One night his mother took us to eat Chinese (something I couldn't imagine doing in front of my family), and as I piled my plate high with fried rice, sesame chicken, and crab rangoon, his sister, who was around eleven at the time, tilted her head and asked thoughtfully, "Mom, why do we pay for Whitney's food if she's just going to throw it up?" It was the kind of straightforward question kids ask that has the ability to silence a room. Shawn later told me he had confided in his mother about my problem, desperately looking for some solution to offer me.

I was caught off guard by his sister's observation and realized that my secret behavior was maybe not-so-secret, but I was pleased for the first time with my weight, and had sacrificed so much to get there. Just three months into my junior year I had managed to lose almost thirty pounds, and each morning I

The smallest I was in high school—130 pounds (2000).

willed the needle on my bathroom scale to go below 130 (spoiler: it never did).

For more than a decade afterward I used 130 pounds—my lowest adult weight—as my goal weight. It's a number that has held seemingly magical properties and the promise of instant happiness. Never mind that I was amphetamine-addicted, starving, and purging—I finally felt like I was *almost* thin enough. Sure, my butt and thighs were still bigger than I wanted, and, yes, my BMI of 23.8 put me dangerously close to 25, which would classify me as overweight (again), but for a brief moment in time, I was satisfied with my overall appearance. Plus, I could fit in my size 9 jeans.

That spring break, a girlfriend and I drove down to Myrtle Beach, which was a noteworthy feat considering GPS hadn't been invented yet, and her mom had given us directions with prompts like "Turn left where the Walmart used to be before the hurricane knocked it down." Somehow, we made it there and let ourselves into her grandmother's swanky condo, prepared for a week of underage drinking and sunbathing. She had brought some bikinis, bikini-short bottoms, and tube tops, and urged me to try them on. I wiggled into them and let her take some photos of me on the balcony with my disposable camera, but I was so dissatisfied with my appearance that I vowed not to go on the beach at all. She tried to convince me, unsuccessfully, so we finally compromised: I would wear a bathing suit on the beach, but with my overalls on top. I spent the days hiding under that outfit in the sun, and nights drinking Zima and making drunken phone calls home to Shawn. I also bought a small turtle, who I named Cappy, on the boardwalk one night, after learning from the seller that, like a goldfish, he most likely wouldn't have a long life in captivity. Fifteen years later, and long after developing the photos of me on the balcony, I am surprised about two things: (1) I actually looked amazing in that tube top and bikini-short combo, and (2) Cappy is still alive and kicking (swimming?).

In keeping with the national average, I lost my virginity at age seventeen, within the safe confines of my first loving relationship. When I confessed to my mom that I was going to have sex with Shawn, she took it fairly well, but still feigned dismay.

"Whitney, you are not . . ."

My tube top and bikini-short combo (2001).

"Mom, yes I am. I already skipped school to go to Planned Parenthood."

(Gasp) "Whitney, you did not!"

"Yes, I did, Mom."

(Pause) "Did they put you in the stirrups?"

"MOM!"

On the scheduled we're-gonna-lose-our-virginity day, I went to the local pharmacy for condoms, spermicide, and gum (in order of importance, naturally), and met up with Shawn. We were both nervous, but I was entirely comfortable with him. Besides loving me wholeheartedly, he made me feel beautiful and appreciated. He was the perfect person with whom to experience first love and all the awkward, confusing, electrifying feelings that come with it. Not only was Shawn distraught over the war I waged with my body, he actively worked to change it. There was never a minute I spent in his presence when he neglected to tell me how stunning I was or how much he loved me. He was the kind of guy who persuaded me to let him see my nakedness in the daylight but relented the second he sensed I was uncomfortable.

A month later I checked another rite of passage off my list, this time without Shawn. Even though he and I were still dating, he had no interest in going to the prom. I didn't want to miss the prom experience altogether, so I invited a good male friend from my theatre company (with Shawn's blessing) and set off with my mom to the local department stores to hunt for a dress. Unlike most girls my age, I had always detested shopping for clothes. The stress brought on by trying to find a perfect pair of jeans made me huff with frustration. I could easily wear a small or medium in almost any top, but my jean size fluctuated tremendously. The biggest size I bought in high school was a 12 from Express. I didn't realize at the time that 12/14 is the beginning of the plus-size range—and thank God for my ignorance, as it surely would have induced another self-imposed starvation period. I didn't like the way waistbands clung to my stomach, leaving red marks in their wake, and how they felt tight around my thighs. I much preferred to wear dance pants (the prefat Whitney equivalent of my present-day spandex) and comfortable T-shirts. However, the formal attire for prom is a rigid standard, so I zigzagged in between the clothing racks looking for the perfect dress. I thought most of them were too garish, with panels of sparkling sequins and ruffles, and my mother thought most of them were too revealing, with considerable cutouts in the midsection and plunging necklines.

Finally, I found a coral pink halter dress with minimal beading on the bust. It looked simple, elegant, and beautiful. I took it with me into the dressing room and removed my clothes. Standing there in front of the mirror, sweating, I analyzed every inch of my body, and it took only seconds for the disgust to wash over me. I noticed every imperfection, from my fleshy, untoned stomach to the dimples and wrinkles on my thighs, all amplified beneath the unforgiving fluorescent light of the dressing room. I shook my head wondering how I'd ever thought I could be satisfied with my body, and overwhelmed by the fact that I had no time to fix it. I didn't even know *how* I could fix it. (Word to the wise: cellulite is totally normal and probably never goes away. Give up obsessing over it now.) I slipped the dress over my head and emerged from the dressing room. My mom clasped her hands under her chin and said I looked beautiful. While I certainly didn't believe her, I couldn't stand the thought of trying on more dresses, so we bought the pink one and headed home.

On the Friday of prom most girls left school early, clocking in a half-day to allow them time to apply acrylic nails and get their hair professionally swept into fancy up-dos. My mother wouldn't have paid for me to get fake nails at my age, and I had an important rehearsal that afternoon anyway, so I stuck it out at school the whole day and then frantically showered, straightened my shoulder-length hair, and applied the little bit of drugstore makeup that I was comfortable with. Once I was completely outfitted with a gold pendant and some expensive rings borrowed from my mom, I actually felt halfway pretty in my dress. My date came over, my dad conducted an impromptu photo shoot, and then we left to make our reservation at a fancy restaurant. When my dad smiled and shook his head, telling me I looked just like my mother, I knew he was proud of me.

At dinner I had a pasta dish and immediately felt my full abdomen pushing against the constriction of my dress. I went to the bathroom and vomited on cue. It had been years since I had to resort to sticking anything down my throat; just clenching my stomach muscles would do the trick, and I was careful to be more controlled than usual to avoid splashing on my dress. When I left the stall, I ran a tissue underneath my watery eyes to clean up my eyeliner and my date and I set off for the dance.

Since neither of us was drinking or doing anything crazy, we didn't want to stay the entire night. After an hour, we gathered

*Prom night, just before throwing up my dinner and
being crowned Prom Princess (2002).*

our things and walked out to the lobby, then I heard my name echoing from the sound system. We ventured back to the dance floor just in time to hear me being crowned Prom Princess. It was especially surprising because I wasn't even aware votes had been cast for such a thing—it happened in homeroom when I was already at Weaver. I was given a sash and tiara, and some girls in the front row were booing, but I was delighted with this unexpected turn of events.

When I woke up the next day, it was my eighteenth birthday, and my parents placed some gifts, balloons, and an obligatory cat card on the patio table outside. After I opened them, Shawn picked me up and we went to a local tattoo parlor so I could get my belly button pierced. Keep in mind, this was 2002, when "I'm a Slave 4 U"–era Britney Spears was all the rage and navel rings were still in fashion. When we got to the tattoo shop, I lay down outstretched on a table as the piercer wiped alcohol across my midsection. Shawn, in his usual supportive fashion, stood at my side, holding my hand with the iron grip of a man who was about to become a father, instead of the calm attentiveness of a boyfriend in a tattoo shop. I was much less troubled with the pain and more concerned with what the guy thought of my bare belly. I looked up at him sheepishly and said, "I'm sorry," as he slid the needle through my skin. Today, I am not embarrassed about my stomach, but horrified by the need I had to apologize for it all those years ago.

Around this time I got a frenzied phone call from Todd, who was playing Kenickie in his high school's production of *Grease*. He breathlessly told me that, a week away from opening night, they had no choreography and no one to play Cha-Cha. I added yet another task to my overwhelming responsibilities and drove out to his school each afternoon to teach choreography to the cast and step in to play the part of Cha-Cha to Todd's Kenickie. (If this doesn't seal his status as Eternal Dance Partner, what does?) It was through this endeavor that I met his girlfriend,

Heather. (No, you're not confused. Yes, Todd, who you watch on *My Big Fat Fabulous Life,* is gay, and yes, he was dating a girl at the time.) Neither Heather nor I particularly liked each other—she tells me that one day I scolded Todd for hanging out with her instead of me, saying, "Bros and Whitney before hos." I don't recall this incident, but I'll take her word for it. There are so many things wrong with it, the most upsetting of which is my usage of the word "hos," but we live and we learn, right?

By opening night, Heather had changed her tune about me. When asked why, she described a moment during rehearsal where I was ranting about people saying "I *could* care less." It was our shared obsession with this grammatical error (it's "I *couldn't* care less," for crying out loud!) that turned her on to me. During curtain call, she presented me with flowers and a huge poster signed by the cast, which my dad had matted and framed. It was the beginning of our lifelong friendship, and saving the day at Todd's school is one of my father's proudest moments even now. He often starts his famous talks with, "It's just like that poster . . ." That's how I know it's going to be a good one.

With another success under my metaphorical belt (y'all know I don't do belts), I eagerly awaited graduation. My parents invited my extended family over for a party. Mom set up the dining room table with different mementos from high school. There were soccer trophies from championships my dad had coached me to, framed awards I'd won, and, of course, my Prom Princess crown. When I think back on my graduation party, I could never recount how many validating and adoring comments my parents expressed to me that night. There has never been a shortage of positive reinforcement or love in the Thore household. My parents think I am the best human being on the planet, and I think the same is true of them. I'm sure my mom complimented my outfit and I'm sure that my dad gave a speech about all my accomplishments, but the thing that sticks out the most to me all these years later about that particular night is a casual remark my mother made: she reminded me to suck in my stomach. I had purchased a knee-length floral skirt and a sleeveless top that zipped down to reveal my nonexistent cleavage. Looking at that photo now, I can't believe anyone would be worried about whether I was sucking in or not. I know that my mother meant no harm, as she'd been sucking in her own stomach longer than I'd been alive. Nevertheless, the constant reminder to appear thinner than I was didn't help me feel confident or attractive. And it made it difficult to breathe.

After graduation was over, Heather, Todd, Tal, and I all performed in another community theatre musical, *Kiss Me, Kate*, while Shawn worked on the crew. I was cast in the ensemble, but I had the distinction of being named dance captain. For one of the numbers, a popular song called "It's Too Darn Hot," the girls were required to wear corsets with a robe layered on top. I found myself in the same dressing room where I'd tried on my prom dress, cursing my body in exactly the same way. By the time we were in dress rehearsals, I was still bitter about having to wear it, and as I stood backstage, the mother of one of the leads walked by me and then turned on her heel.

"Whitney," she said critically, "you ought to close that robe up so you're not hanging all out there." I didn't have breasts to speak of, so I knew she meant my body, and her disparaging remark cut me. In a bout of defiance, I decided I would keep my robe open, like the other girls, unless I was told by my director otherwise. I never was asked to close it up, and onstage I cocked my hip and bounced my butt as hard as I could, making sure *every* single thing was hanging out.

I'm glad that her comment incited disobedience in me rather than deference, but I have to wonder why we as women take such comments to heart in the first place. This woman made a thoughtless observation that should have had no impact on me, but here I am, still remembering it. How many random, thoughtful compliments had I refused to accept that hadn't made it past my fortress of self-disgust? How many beautiful things have I forgotten or simply not had room to store?

The best thing to come out of that summer was my friendship with Heather, which is as strong today, more than a decade later, as it was then. Driving home from rehearsal one day, she asked if I would stop at Wendy's. I never bought fast food for myself, likely out of habit because I didn't eat much fast food growing up. There was the occasional Sunday fast-food brunch after my brother and I attended church with my dad, and the extremely rare instance my mother picked up McDonald's for dinner. So when Heather requested a cheeseburger, I obliged and even ordered something for myself, but as we pulled out onto the street going toward my house, I cut into a darkened auto parts store parking lot.

"Do you mind if we eat here?" I asked, handing her the french fries.

"No . . . why?" she asked.

"I just don't want to eat this in front of my parents," I explained, and so we sat there in the empty parking lot, eating our Wendy's meals in solidarity, away from anyone who could scold or judge me for doing so.

A few days later Mom and I were prowling the aisles of Target, picking out a new bedspread and closet organizers, as college was closing in fast. I had decided to join my brother at Appalachian State. My dad worked tirelessly building me a bookshelf to place on top of my desk. (He procured the dorm room furniture measurements from the school and set out to build a bookcase that would include a shelf to accommodate my turtle Cappy's aquarium—in case anyone is confused about how much this man loves me.) On the day of the move Shawn came over and helped my dad load everything into the car, and then followed us up the winding mountain roads to Boone. I rode in the packed car with my dad, and Shawn took my mom in his Jeep. As we rounded curves and our ears started popping, my dad cleared his throat and launched into one of his father-daughter talks, listing all my accomplishments and reasons why he was so proud of me (like the poster). Then he grabbed my hand in his.

"There are a couple things I wish we'd had some more progress with before you went off to school," he said. I raised my eyebrows to ask him what they were. "I wish I'd introduced you more to religion, and I wish you'd lost some more weight." Then he flashed a comforting smile. "But there's still plenty of time for those two things, so no big deal."

I wonder now, fourteen years later, if my dad could have imagined that I still wouldn't have made the progress we wanted with weight loss, that it *is* a big deal, and that as a thirty-two-year-old woman, I'd be writing a book about why.

5

PCOS DIDN'T MAKE ME *THIS* FAT

Moving into my college dorm was more hectic than back-to-school commercials ever led me to believe, and it was also more extraordinary. I dug my toes into my new pink, purple, and turquoise–patterned rug, feeling like I was standing on the precipice of the unknown rather than in a thirteen-by-seventeen-foot box with hideous tiled floor and radiator heating. In the moment it took Shawn and my parents to reach the stairwell, I witnessed both an amicable end to my first relationship and the advent of my independence.

On the first day of classes, adrenaline stirred me awake before the sun, and I sprung out of bed and charged to the communal shower down the hall. I carefully straightened my hair and dressed in the outfit I'd chosen the night before. (The only time in my entire life, I think, that I've managed to do this.) My course load consisted of the usual freshman classes as well as an advanced dance class to which I'd gained special admission. I also attended auditions for the main stage theatre production, which freshman typically had zero chances of being cast in. The monologue I delivered went better than I'd hoped, and there

My first day of freshman year at App State (2002).

were whispers going around about "Hunter's little sister." The director even invited me to callbacks just to tell me how impressed he was. My first week at App State was an indisputable success—with a fast-approaching expiration date.

No more than a few weeks into the semester, I had already fallen behind in all my classes. Most professors instituted a three-unexcused-absence policy, and I used up all my days right away. Contrary to the first day of school, when I had popped out of bed with ambition and ease, I often found it hard to get out of bed at all.

Prior to college, my sweet father had woken me up every single school day of my life. And not just once—he would let me "hit snooze," and he'd return to my room in ten-minute increments until I was up. Sometimes I was so exhausted that I turned on the shower, undressed, wrapped my hair in a towel, and lay down in the adjacent carpeted room with the sinks to sleep for seven more minutes while I faked a shower. Of course, my dad wasn't in my dorm (and thank God for that, really) to wake me up each morning, and I found it nearly impossible to be roused by an alarm.

Nothing could cajole me out of bed—not even the three separate alarm clocks I strategically placed at the other end of the room so I'd have to physically get up to shut them off. Some-

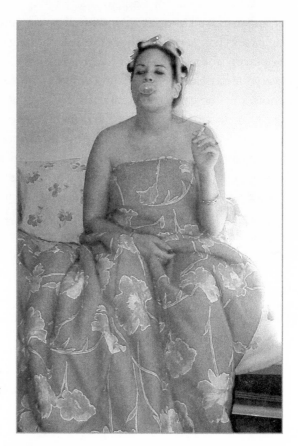

Before everything went to shit (2002).

times my roommate, Margo, would come back from class mid-morning bewildered to find me still in bed. She'd swear I'd gotten up in the morning to turn my alarm off and sometimes even had mumbled conversations with her as she was leaving. I *did* have a history of sleepwalking, but I never could figure out if I was actually waking up in the mornings or not. All I knew was I couldn't remember any of it, I was oversleeping every day, and, consequently, my grades were plummeting.

My dance class was the only glimmer of light I had left, but even it wasn't safe from my self-destruction. By the end of September, just a month into my collegiate career, I noticed I was putting on weight. My jeans were strangling my thighs and my stomach looked pudgier when I lifted up my shirts. I chalked it up to my change in lifestyle, as I wasn't dancing every single day or playing soccer anymore. I had a prepaid meal card like most everyone on campus, so I didn't always make the healthiest choices in the cafeteria. I'd started drinking at parties and I'd gone to the campus nurse to get birth control pills, too. The year before, when I'd secured birth control before having sex with Shawn, I'd opted for Depo-Provera, the birth control shot that's super effective but notoriously causes weight gain. I didn't need anything else that would impede weight loss, so I swapped the shot for pills. One night after I'd purged a late-night meal that I'd shared with a guy I was dating, I became paranoid that I'd thrown up my birth control pill as well. Although neither outcome was appealing, I knew I'd rather be fat than pregnant, so I stopped throwing up my food. On top of that, I no longer had easy access to Adderall. There was one girl on my hall who had sold me some, but after taking a pill in hopes of catching up on some schoolwork, I lay awake for hours in bed with heart palpitations that sent me into an anxiety attack and caused me to call my mother, who patiently stayed on the phone with me while I tried to articulate why I thought I was dying. I swore off Adderall after that, and to this day I've never taken it again.

These seemingly minor changes amounted to major problems in dance class, when I was confronted twice a week with a mirrored image of myself that seemed to swell more every day. Sometimes when I looked at the class in the mirror, it took me a second too long to identify my reflection, and when I did, it startled me, almost as if I'd caught a glimpse of an intruder. I started to loathe the sight of myself so much that I fixed my attention on the wall just above the top of the mirrors, causing my professors to constantly correct my focus and tell me to bring my chin down. It wasn't long before I couldn't bear to attend my dance class at all. My body felt awkward and uneasy, like when you're trying to sleep on a long car ride and you can't get comfortable, no matter how you twist and turn.

I could feel the black cloud seeping back in, and I withdrew. I began discovering mysterious black and purple bruises on my body, covering my hips and the outsides of my thighs. I racked my brain to figure out why I was becoming so clumsy—I was regularly banging into doorways or hitting the back of my desk chair as I entered my room. I was losing my balance a lot, too, but I never felt dizzy. Then I had an epiphany: my body was ballooning so dramatically and so fast that I frequently misjudged my own size in relation to my surroundings. It wasn't that I was accident-prone; it was that I had lost kinesthetic awareness of my body. The impact of that thought walloping me on the head hurt worse than any of the collisions with furniture. My body was physically careening out of control, and of course, each time the number on the scale went up, I slunk further down into depression.

My first report card was a string of D's, one C, and a glaring F in my dance class. These kinds of grades were unheard of for me and I tried to explain to my father that I was depressed, and I promised I would get better.

The summer before college, my mother had confided in me that a year earlier she had attempted suicide by closing the garage door and turning on the car. She described being in the throes of a particularly grim period of depression and reasoned that she could just "go to sleep." After several minutes passed, she looked down at the clock on the dashboard and saw that it was three-twenty. The realization that I would be home at three-thirty and find her dead, propelled her out of the car. She'd struggled with depression her entire life, and this was the incident that finally spurred her to seek help. She was prescribed Prozac, and while it didn't cure her depression, it did make a marked difference. She told me she was divulging this information because she feared that I was depressed and she didn't want me to suffer in silence for as long as she had. After learning this sobering news, my brother got the number 320 tattooed on his leg, and I got a prescription for antidepressants. I vowed to my dad that if I just took my medicine regularly, everything would work itself out. I had no logical explanation as to why taking my medicine seemed like an insurmountable task, but it's something that I *still* deal with to this day.

I knew the letter notifying my parents that I was on academic probation would be coming to the house, and I convinced my mother to vigilantly watch the mailbox for it and to hide it when it came. I promised her after next semester I'd be off academic probation, so there was no need for Dad to know.

"You know how upset he'll be," I told her. "You know how heartbroken he'll be." The sigh on the other end of the phone let me know she agreed.

By the time I went home for Christmas break, I had packed on more than three times the amount of weight that college freshmen are reasonably expected to gain. I met Shawn for dinner

Fifty pounds heavier than the start of college, wearing a maternity dress (2003).

A rare photo of me at the end of my freshman year—officially fat— with my parents at my brother's graduation (2003).

and tried to joke about how I'd gained the "Freshman Fifty" instead of the "Freshman Fifteen," but I wasn't kidding about the pounds; I had literally gained fifty. I needed new clothes badly and I hadn't the slightest idea where to shop for them. I found myself at Target, fingering the maternity clothes with elastic waistbands and generous flowing fabric that could accommodate and conceal my growing circumference. When my mom saw the purchases hanging in my closet, she urged me to cut out the tags lest anyone else see them, and as if snipping out the evidence would make the problem go away.

When I returned to school in the spring, I chopped my hair off and pierced my nose, in what seems like, in hindsight, a feeble attempt to regain some control over my appearance. When my parents visited App State to see a one-act play I'd been cast in (to this day, they've never missed a performance), my dad scoffed at my new nose ring, saying that maybe my facial piercing would be easier to handle if I'd lose some weight.

I wanted to lose weight more than anything I'd *ever* wanted, but I didn't know how I could lose weight while I was still actively gaining it with every passing second. I was so ashamed when I went to get a new student ID card after losing mine and the ladies at the desk spent minutes comparing me to the image on their computer screens taken just four months prior. They were not able to grasp that I was, in fact, that same person. Finally, I referenced that I'd gained a lot of weight and I wasn't trying to trick them.

The two women, out of pity, pretended to be shocked. "Oh, *no*, honey, it's not that. It just that . . . your hair is so much shorter now!"

I missed more classes than I attended. I always declined when my friends invited me to a drive on the parkway or to hang around outside on a pretty day. I watched from my bed as they rushed sororities and I slept and drank myself into oblivion every weekend. Each time I woke up, my affliction was still there, like a throbbing, full-body hangover. I ached and oozed self-hatred from every stretched pore. And it wasn't even just my weight anymore—the rest of my physical appearance was deteriorating, too. My hair started thinning out, and just running my fingers through my scalp would produce a handful of tangled strands. Coarse black hairs started poking through the surface of my neck and chin, and distinct, horizontal grooves showed up on my nails.

I spent the summer after freshman year at home. The issue of my weight gain was not explicitly discussed by my parents or by friends; it was too touchy and taboo an issue, so everyone tiptoed around it. I was the 200-pound elephant in everyone's room. At my request, my dad purchased me a membership for the remodeled YMCA complete with a sauna and swimming pool. He even bought an additional membership so that I could bring someone with me whenever I wanted. My dad may not have always said the right thing to me, but I could always count on him to show up when I needed him. Even though I swam regularly that summer, when I moved back up to school—this time to my own apartment—I clocked in at 230 pounds. I was absolutely horrified to be *100* pounds over my goal weight.

My new room had no windows, so I quite literally spent much of my time in darkness. If I'd found it hard to function while living on campus, living in my own apartment made it damn near impossible. I still couldn't wake up for class, but I started having lucid dreams each morning. In them, I was on campus living life, and fulfilling responsibilities, but then I'd wake up huddled under my covers in blackness and half the day would be gone.

Exacerbating my hopelessness was the fact that I'd never learned to cook or care for myself. I ordered pizza a lot, not because I couldn't resist it, but because it saved me from having to claw myself out of my depression and go into the world. Cooking is a learned skill, but for me, self-care was, too. I'd never realized it until I was on my own, but waking up and feeding myself and taking a shower even if I wasn't going anywhere was not instinctual for me. Forget swallowing pills or doing anything other than the bare minimum. If it required more than brushing my teeth, you can bet it felt overwhelming. I found myself always asking, "What's the point?" Nothing held significance anymore.

After my first semester, I was so depressed and doing so poorly in my classes that I couldn't fathom the thought of continuing my education. I could transfer to UNCG and live at home, I thought. I needed unconditional love. I needed help. I needed my parents.

I looked up transfer information on the UNCG website only to find that my GPA wasn't high enough to transfer. Who was I? A year earlier I graduated with honors and awards and distinctions, and now I couldn't even transfer schools? I called my dad and confessed to him that I was nonfunctional. What he said to me was incredibly surprising. He said I could come home if I wanted to and take a break from school. He said—and this was the biggest shocker: "You don't ever have to go back to school if you don't want to. But promise me you'll give this semester a shot. Just do your best on your exams. And we'll figure it out after." Hearing my dad say this was such an immense comfort. I reckon now that he was remembering my mother sitting by herself in a running car in the garage, and he thought that tough love wasn't the best approach to take with me. So I gave school another shot just to appease my dad. Two years later I had raised my GPA enough to earn a spot on the dean's list. I was in no way living up to my potential, but I had become more accepting of my identity—the introverted, nondancer who people ignored.

In the fall of my first year in college, I went to a theatre party and ended up talking to a shy, handsome guy I'd never seen before. Afterward, it became evident he had a knack for turning up everywhere I happened to be. I finally learned that his name was Eric, and we began spending all our time together. He met my parents and I met his. I fell in love with him swiftly and without reservation. Soon after our relationship began, I was using his computer when I saw a minimized conversation on the screen between Eric and a friend. I maximized the conversation without really thinking and saw that Eric was chatting with his friend about me and had sent him some photos, but I didn't recognize the person in them. The girl in the photos was younger and thinner. In one photo, she stood poised holding a gray cat, wearing jeans that couldn't have been bigger than a size 10. In another she gave a toothy grin to the camera with her auburn-ish hair spilling over her face that had no hint of a double chin. In the last one, taken during a dance performance, she was pictured mid-arabesque, a black-and-white cinched-waist silhouette with lean, elegantly positioned arms. Eric had ripped these photos of a sixteen-, seventeen-, and eighteen-year-old me from my private photo website and passed them off as his current girlfriend.

Not even a month later, right after Thanksgiving, he left his email open on my computer. As I went to close it, the words "love doctor" jumped out at me. First I assumed it was spam, but something told me to open it. I realized that it wasn't spam and that it was tied to an actual online-dating account. It's an old one, I reassured myself. He was probably on a dating website while he was single. I clicked to access the account. As I scrolled through, looking at a mostly empty in-box and totally empty sent box, I started to relax, but then I got a rush of adrenaline. His profile photo was one I had taken of him. The kicker? I'd showed it to him and cooed, "This is THE best photo of you ever in existence."

I printed out all the evidence and went to pick Eric up from class. I'd planned to wait until we got home to confront him, but he demanded to know what was wrong, so I pulled over and handed him the stapled pages. He said what I figured he would, that he wasn't on the site to actually talk to people and that he hadn't communicated with anyone. I told him that what bothered me more was why he needed validation from random women on the Internet. He apologized and cried at the idea of losing me, and I decided to trust Eric and stay with him. Aside from these upsetting instances, he was an affectionate and devoted boyfriend and I fell more deeply in love with him than anyone I'd known before.

Eric and I talked about getting married, in a *that's far off* kind of way, but then one night we were lying in bed and he asked me what I would say if he asked me right then.

"Are you asking me right now?"

"I guess I am."

Guided by my instinct, which told me that finding a man I loved who wanted to marry me was akin to a miracle, I answered, "I would say yes." The next day we started looking for a ring. It was all a bit surreal, but I felt no resistance in my heart, and even my friends and family didn't think we were *totally* crazy. We found a ring, white gold with a yellow sapphire and microscopic diamonds, for $300 on eBay. When it came to the post office, we went to pick it up and I was overjoyed that it fit, since I'd assumed I would have to have it resized.

It may not have been a romantic proposal, but Eric had subtle ways of making me feel loved. He always cooked for me, and after every meal he would always ask me, "Did you get enough?" That one little question always made me feel so cared for. One day he made an offhand comment, something like, "You don't eat that much." I don't? I thought, relieved. I weighed 280 pounds. I must have gotten that way because I was an overeating slob, and surely everyone else thought the same thing. To hear Eric say he didn't think I ate too much was like a pardon from a king.

I had developed serious neuroses regarding food. Now that I, for once in my life, wasn't on some kind of formal diet, I had the staggering revelation that I had absolutely no clue how to eat like a normal person. Did normal people really eat three times a day? I always deprived myself of food until I was famished—even if food was available to me when I woke up, I wouldn't eat it until my stomach ached with hunger. Once, before I'd started dating Eric, I'd starved for almost twenty-four hours when I finally resorted to making a box of macaroni and cheese on the stove. By the time it was done, I was so ravenous that I ate the entire pot standing up while it was still sitting on the burner. A half hour later, I began having chest pains that got so severe I called my parents, who happened to be in town for the weekend, and they took me to the emergency room. The doctor appeared puzzled when he asked me what I'd had to eat that day and I made up something I thought a "normal" person would have had. It wasn't until a few minutes later when I inadvertently threw up a box of half-digested macaroni and cheese all over the floor that he diagnosed the pain as air in my chest from eating too fast. I don't think I've ever been more mortified in my life as when he looked at me knowingly with big eyes and said in an exaggerated fashion, as if he were talking to a child: "Sloooow dooooown."

To avoid the inevitable judgment of others, I was accustomed to eating alone, and when I had to do it in public, say at dinner with family or friends, I would fill up on something before I went, so that I could just pick at a salad in front of other people. I never wanted to be the fat girl who *had* to eat, and I went to great lengths to hide it. If I went through a drive-thru, all I could think about was how disgusting and lazy I must look, so if I ordered a combo, I'd also ask for a second drink different from my own (the same drink could just look like an extra for me!) to give the illusion that maybe two people were splitting the meal.

My weird behavior that revolved around food kept me on edge constantly. One day my roommate offered me a slice of the homemade red velvet birthday cake her mom had left on our kitchen counter. I, of course, declined, but when I came home hours later, tipsy after a night out, the untouched cake was irresistible to my empty stomach. I took out a knife from the drawer and cut myself a small slice. Then I cut myself another. It was so good that when I stopped chewing, I realized I'd eaten half of my roommate's cake. There was no way for me to explain this away and I couldn't replace it with a store-bought cake without being found out. I was so afraid of what my roommate would think of me if she came home to see that I'd indulged in three times more than the slice she offered me. Panicky, I looked at the clock—it was after two A.M., the bars were closed, and I knew she'd be home soon. I had to do *something* fast. In a stroke of desperation, or perhaps brilliance, I picked up the glass plate that held the cake and slammed it down onto the kitchen floor, watching it break into huge, jagged shards. Then I smeared icing and cake on the floor, swept the glass into the trash can, and transferred the fallen cake remnants to a plastic bag I disposed of in the dumpster. I cleaned up the kitchen about three-quarters of the way and scrawled a note to my roommate:

> I am SO sorry girl! I'm a little too drunk and I knocked your cake off the counter. Watch out for glass. I'll mop in the morning and buy you any cake you want. I am SO SORRY!!!!

With my feet still in the stirrups, the nurse practitioner at my OBGYN's office, Liz, sat on a little wheeled stool, furrowing her brow over my medical records. Then she said something that would change my life.

"I think you have PCOS."

I had never heard those four letters put together and had no idea what they meant. Liz gave me some pamphlets, scheduled some tests, and sent me on my way. When I got to my car, I started thumbing through the glossy pages with photos of smiling women and their families. I was quickly overwhelmed with information as I scanned the major takeaways on the disorder: words like *fertility, insulin, risks, no cure, androgens, weight gain*. I learned that PCOS (polycystic ovary syndrome) is an endocrine disorder that affects one out of ten American women. It was a syndrome with no cure, marked by sudden and severe weight gain, difficulty losing weight, infertility, irregular periods, acne, thinning hair, and excessive facial and body hair. As I pored over the literature, my heart started beating faster. Everything I was reading sounded just like me.

I drove to my parents' house in a blur. I spread the pamphlets out on the kitchen table to show my mom. I started Googling. Within minutes I got scared: it seemed like my diagnosis was less of an explanation and more of a warning. The statistics were harrowing: more than fifty percent of women with PCOS will have diabetes or prediabetes before the age of forty; the risk of heart attack is four to seven times higher than in women not affected by PCOS; women with PCOS have greater risk of high blood pressure, high "bad" cholesterol, and low "good" cholesterol; and PCOS is linked to endometrial cancer, sleep apnea, anxiety, and depression. As if that wasn't enough, I read on, women with PCOS have higher rates of miscarriage, gestational diabetes, preeclampsia, and premature delivery, *if* they do succeed at becoming pregnant. I looked at Mom as the gravity of this disorder hit me.

"Does this mean I can't have kids?" I whispered.

"I don't know, honey," she said. Then she shook her head. "No, I'm sure it doesn't mean that."

That night, I called Eric and told him the news that there was this horrible disorder and my doctor thought I had it. He tried his best to console me, mostly reminding me that I hadn't been officially diagnosed and might not have it at all.

"Would you still marry me if I can't have kids?" I asked, my voice wavering.

"Yes," he promised. "I will still marry you."

As I drove back up to the mountains that night, I considered all the possibilities and felt a range of emotions. On the one hand, I was relieved—this was quite possibly an answer for all the questions I'd had for years about what was going on with my body. I also felt angry. Why was I just finding this out? Why had I never heard of PCOS before? Why did it take this long for a medical professional to wonder whether I might have it? Why had all my previous questions been ignored? Each time I'd asked my doctor why I kept missing my periods, I was told I was just young and irregular. Each time I'd gotten on a scale, my weight gain was dismissed and attributed to college, or birth control, or Prozac, or drinking. I'd never even known who to tell about the handfuls of hair that came out every time I ran my palm through my ponytail, the black, coarse hairs that had begun popping up on my chin (a result of too much testosterone), or the ridges on my nails (evidence of insulin dysfunction). After all of this frustration I realized that perhaps PCOS had been the reason I'd uncontrollably packed on the pounds starting as soon as I got to college.

Sure, my drinking, food choices, depression, and inactivity were partly to blame, but I spiraled into those patterns only because I'd gained 100 pounds so quickly and seemingly out of nowhere in the first few months of college. Now, realizing I might be suffering from PCOS, I tried, for just a second, to wrap my head around the idea that maybe there was a medical issue at play. Maybe I wasn't simply lazy and disgusting and inherently broken. But I'd been beating myself up for as long as I could remember and I didn't have any more space to let another idea inside.

A few weeks later I returned to Greensboro for my tests. In order to rule out Hashimoto's disease, thyroid problems, and even a benign brain tumor, I underwent test after test. Everything was negative. Liz explained that there is no definitive test to diagnose PCOS, but that I had some telltale symptoms like chronic anovulation (lack of periods) and hyperandrogenism (an excess of male hormones, like testosterone). After the tests indicated that I was insulin resistant, I was officially diagnosed with PCOS. (I wouldn't have an ultrasound until I was thirty-one, lying on my back in a specialist's office as he counted my ovarian cysts, approximately thirty in total.)

Since the diagnosis raised many more questions than it provided answers, my dad helped me find a well-respected endocrinologist in Greensboro and I headed back home for the appointment. My parents accompanied me into the doctor's office. We were all nervous and counting on him, hoping that when we left, I'd know exactly what I needed to do to beat this thing. But it didn't have a cure—was "beating it" even possible?

My first impression of the doctor was dismal. After recounting nearly a decade of periods, weights, and other various symptoms, I lay down on his table to undergo a physical examination. He worked his way down my body, starting with the lymph nodes under my jaw, and when he got to my stomach, he lifted up my shirt. "Do you shave the hair on your stomach?" he asked. "No, I don't have any excessive body hair," I reminded him, annoyed that he didn't remember from earlier in the appointment when I'd given him an overview of my symptoms. Before we left, he wrote a prescription for metformin and another drug, saying, "This should help with the excessive body hair."

My experience with this doctor was unfortunately not unique. Although he'd explained some of the more technical aspects of PCOS, I didn't feel like I'd been listened to as an individual. It so happens that I have every symptom *other* than excessive body hair. Because PCOS is a grouping of symptoms, each woman can have a different combination of them. It's possible, for instance, for some women with PCOS to get regular periods, and a third of women diagnosed with PCOS have never struggled with their weight.

Disappointed with my doctor, I returned to my apartment with some pills and a lot of confusion. I was not alone in this. *U.S. News & World Report Health** describes PCOS as a "silent disorder that wreaks havoc on the body," and sheds light on the emotional toll of PCOS. Part of that article reads as follows:

> *Gretchen Kubacky, one of the few psychologists in the nation who specializes in PCOS, assists women dealing with the "emotional fallout" of having the condition. Many have been struggling with infertility, weight gain, hormone imbalances, and other medical issues for years without a definitive diagnosis.*
>
> *"By the time they get to my office, many show signs of depression," Kubacky says. Depression is four times more common in women with PCOS, and a third of all women with PCOS meet the criteria for major depression, she says. They are also more likely to experience anxiety, low self-esteem, suicidal thoughts, and eating disorders.*
>
> *Many struggle with poor body image. "They have facial hair, male pattern balding, and hair on their body where it doesn't belong. Many are significantly overweight. This is not the American ideal of what a woman should [look] like. The body shaming is sort of a micro aggression that gradually erodes a person's psyche," Kubacky says.*
>
> *The lack of awareness among medical practitioners compounds the problem. "There's a lot of blame in the medical arena. Doctors who aren't aware of PCOS think people just can't control themselves or aren't working hard enough to lose weight.*

---

* health.usnews.com/health-news/patient-advice/articles/2015/07/27/polycystic -ovary-syndrome-the-silent-disorder-that-wreaks-havoc-on-the-body

Yet these women exercise and diet constantly, and they still weigh 200 pounds."

I was battling so many feelings, and outrage was right at the top—outrage at the people, the syndrome, the shame that had led me here to this moment, now lying on my carpet in the fetal position, crying over what my twenty-two years of life had become. I yearned to have the body I'd had just four years earlier—the body that society had still told me wasn't good enough, and the body that even I didn't appreciate at the time. I wanted to know why my family had sent me to nutritionists instead of therapists. Why my friends never argued with the fact that I wouldn't wear shorts. Why hadn't someone—anyone—told me I was good enough the way I was?

Sobbing into the carpet and not knowing what to do, I dialed my father. When he answered and heard my muffled tears, he gently asked me what was wrong.

"Daddy," I wailed, "I love you. I want you to know how much I love you. But I think some things have gone wrong." I told my dad how much some of the things from my childhood had affected me. Seemingly innocuous things: my mother's constant refrain of "suck your stomach in," my dad's readiness to find me a nutritionist, his unintentional but hurtful offhand comments that policed my weight and appearance, the magazines that published only thin girls on their pages, the incessant advertisements for weight-loss plans and quick fixes, and the fact that no one seemed to care enough to intervene even through the years when they knew I was in a dangerous cycle of restriction and purging.

One, or even some, of these things might not have derailed the self-worth that I'd like to believe is innate in human beings. But all of these things, coming at me from every direction, had broken down a talented dancer, a soccer champion, a prom princess. They left this twenty-two-year-old woman feeling like a lost child, desperately searching for any kind of assurance that her life was not completely over when she felt with every fiber of her being that it was.

For over an hour my dad listened to me babble almost incoherently about everything in my life that had culminated in this moment. He apologized for his mistakes. He reinforced that all he wanted was for me to be happy. And, as I suspected he would, he promised me everything would be okay. What people don't realize about that statement—"It will be okay"—is that sometimes it won't. And no one tells you that "okay" might not happen for a decade down the road.

Knowing now that I had PCOS, I rededicated myself to making the best of the rest of my college career. I was not on track to graduate in four years, so I planned to graduate in five. I got cast in two main stage productions: once as an authoritative, nasty landlord in Brecht's *The Good Woman of Setzuan,* and the other time as a grandmother in the farce *Moon Over Buffalo.*

I was happy that I had finally secured some success in the theatre department, but it was obvious to me that I'd been cast in those two roles only because they were the kinds of women (old and bossy) who are allowed to be fat. Even though my professors championed "nontraditional" casting, it was apparent every time a cast list went up that this applied to an actor's race and gender, not his or her weight.

I branched out and made some decent friends in the theatre department. I joined the theatre honor society, Alpha Psi Omega. I quit drinking so much. I found a nutritionist who helped deal with my emotional turmoil. I read Buddhist texts and meditated, often driving the Blue Ridge Parkway alone for peace of mind and solace. I was making some solid improvements in my life and my depression was lifting, but that's not to say things were easy.

I had a lot to come to terms with, and PCOS was at the forefront of my mind. I wished I had been diagnosed sooner. I wished that I hadn't been so ashamed to go to doctors and that I'd pushed them to see if there was anything wrong with me as soon as I started gaining weight my freshman year. But I was also disgruntled that no one had noticed or cared about my symptoms, starting from the very first one: the absence of my period. And I knew that PCOS was to blame for my initial weight gain. Sure, most people gain weight their first year of college, but I'd gained a tremendous amount uncontrollably. I felt like I'd been forced to put on a fat suit and go out in public. I had no protection against the insults, the isolation, and the shame. By the time my freshman year had ended, I'd already started going downhill. I'd opted out of my life, preferring to be alone, safe from ridicule. I'd stopped dancing, which stifled my joy. I drank too much. I rarely left my house. Everything I had done to cope had only compounded the problem.

Today, I get criticized often for talking about PCOS. I hear multiple times a day that PCOS isn't even a real disorder or that I must be using it as an excuse because "I/my sister/wife/brother's ex-girlfriend has it and SHE isn't as fat as you." Dealing with misinformed people like this is exhausting.

PCOS made me fat. The inability of insulin to function normally is one reason why women with PCOS tend to gain weight or have a hard time losing weight.*

Did it make me *this* fat? No, I can't say that, but it's not as easy as attributing the first hundred pounds to PCOS and then saying I did all the rest, either. Because insulin resistance com-

---

* www.obesityaction.org/educational-resources/resource-articles-2/obesity-related-diseases/polycystic-ovarian-syndrome-pcos-and-obesity

plicates my body in ways that will not affect a person without insulin resistance, it will *always* be significantly easier for me to gain weight and harder for me to lose it regardless of what I do. Can I pinpoint the exact biological processes that caused the rolls on my back or the flab on my arms? Of course not—and, no, the pizza didn't help matters. But I want to be able to bring attention to this disorder that affects millions of women worldwide without being blasted for "making excuses." Because the truth is, I don't care why anyone is fat, and I don't feel that I need an excuse to exist in my body the way it is now; but I also have a responsibility, as a woman suffering from an underrepresented incurable syndrome, to talk about it and make people listen.

6

AMERICANS AREN'T THE WORST OF THE FAT-SHAMERS

As I slowly came to terms with my PCOS diagnosis, I began to find my footing once again, and after graduating from college, Eric and I decided to take an adventurous next step. A friend of ours named Daryl from the theatre department had left the year before to teach English in Korea, and without any better future plans, Eric and I armed ourselves with a *Lonely Planet* guide and we booked our tickets to do the same. Immediately after landing in Daegu, South Korea, I experienced major sensory overload. The city was an overwhelming landscape of sky-high apartment buildings, brightly lit digital screens, and restaurants sandwiched between shops and PC Bangs (gaming rooms). The sidewalks were crowded with throngs of people, looking like giant, moving amoebas made up of suits, high heels, and school uniforms. Taxis, buses, and cars honked incessantly. My comparatively small-town upbringing had not prepared me for all of the pulsating excitement of urban life, and all the auditory and visual diversions made simply crossing the street could spark a panic attack.

Adding to my general bafflement was the fact that Eric and I did not speak one word of Korean. We didn't know our physical address and we didn't even have a cellphone (this was before iPhones existed). But the most unnerving thing was that in this bustling metropolis of more than 2.5 million citizens, we knew only one person: our college friend, Daryl. I'd done my fair share of traveling in Europe by this point, but knowing that I was not a tourist with a hotel reservation and a ticket back home was discombobulating.

Eric and I began our training at MoonKkang English School, which had eighteen different branches scattered throughout the country. Because MoonKkang was a *hagwon* ("academy" is the closest English translation), students attended after their regular school day between four-thirty and ten-thirty P.M., spending one hour with a foreign teacher and one hour with a Korean counterpart. Students were not allowed to speak Korean in English class, nor were we allowed to speak it to them. The thought of leaving school only to attend *more* school seemed like overkill to me, but this was the norm in Korea, and children often attended two or three different types of academies each day. There were three levels of schools within the MoonKkang system: regular, special, and Young Jae, which my managers described as the "genius school." Since Eric and I would be teaching at a regular branch, the ability to discipline a roomful of rambunctious children whose language we didn't understand would prove more useful than any English expertise.

Our training also doubled as a crash course in cultural sensitivity. We learned never to use the color red to write a student's name on the white board (red is reserved for writing names of the deceased); we were shown how to motion for a student with our palm turned down instead of up (the latter is meant for calling a dog); and we were advised to always use two hands when passing something to an elder or someone in a higher position than ourselves.

Life abroad presented some minor inconveniences, mostly

related to lack of appliances—our apartment had no dishwasher, dryer, or garbage disposal, so we cleaned up after meals the old-fashioned way, hung our clothes up to dry, and composted left-over food. We had a toilet, but many places, including our school, didn't. Instead, it had squatters—porcelain bowls set into the floor—and toilet paper was not to be flushed, but placed in a small trash can within each stall. Maneuvering my 280-pound body into a crouched position and hovering over a squat-ter for the duration of my bathroom experience involved a learning curve that my quads did not appreciate.

There were things that made me scratch my head, like the in-ability (or unwillingness, I wasn't sure which) to line up at the ATM or cash register, the puzzling promotional deals like "Buy one lipstick, get a pack of men's underwear for free," how Kore-ans are considered one year old at birth and everyone turns a year older on January 1 (making a child born in December two years old just one month after they are born), and, perhaps the most disconcerting thing of all, corn on pizza. But for every in-stance of something I found bizarre, there was something else that I thought was genius, like floor heating, twenty-four-hour delivery for practically everything (even fast food), and televi-sions at the dentist's office. Koreans flat-out had the best cus-tomer service I'd ever experienced and the cleanest subway stations I'd ever set foot in, along with some of the most sophis-ticated technology, like the fastest high-speed Internet in the world and high-speed trains I'd never seen the likes of in North America. I even grew to find some of the initially peculiar things endearing, like the way couples wore matching shirts, the way people ate communally, and how hand-holding between friends was normal, regardless of age or gender.

But for all of the positives, there were some striking differ-ences that I couldn't reconcile. For starters, South Korea has a heavy drinking culture, and it was commonplace every morning of the week to stumble over a man passed out on the street curled up in a drunken stupor, still dressed in his suit, spooning with his briefcase. No one seemed to blink when a sloshed man unzipped his pants to relieve himself at a busy crosswalk, shooting urine onto the concrete and narrowly missing pedestrians. Twice I found myself on the street witnessing an inebriated man beating his wife or girlfriend in front of dozens of people who remained unfazed.

And for all of Korea's innovative and progressive leadership in technology, I found the country to be archaic in other ways. Korea was not only extremely ethnocentric, but at times, xenophobic. When Daryl—who is black—and I walked on the streets together, people called out, "Ah-free-ka!" (Africa!) I was shocked one night when I was flipping through channels on the TV and landed on a show featuring Korean performers wearing blackface. My colleagues and students alike regularly spoke ill of the Japanese, and asked me why anyone would want to vacation in "dirty" countries like Vietnam or the Philippines. After a couple of weeks in the country, my parents sent me a care package, and in it was a beautiful, diamond-encrusted heart pendant. My coworker oohed and awed over it, then turned the box over in her hand and gasped. "Oh! Too bad," she giggled, pointing to the small writing on the bottom of the box. "Never mind. It's made in *China*."

I knew before arriving that Koreans were generally quite slim and that I wouldn't be able to purchase any clothes there. One of my first Korean friends was the equivalent of a U.S. size 14 and she bashfully confided in me that she had to shop for men's clothes to find anything that fit her body and that her mother harangued her to lose weight so she could find a husband. Signs and advertisements displaying the country's obsession with plastic surgery were everywhere, broadcasting a belief that anything could (and should) be cosmetically fixed to fit the preferred aesthetic. Beauty standards were different and even more rigid than back home—Koreans wanted pale skin (it was difficult to find makeup or sunscreen without lightening or whitening agents), creased eyelids (many of my teenage students already had "double eyelid" surgery), and slender bodies with an "S-curve" for women.

Despite these unpleasant attributes, Eric and I were determined to make it our home, so we settled into our tiny apartment and bought a Persian kitten from a pet shop downtown. We named him Henry-Kimchi, a nod to Korean cuisine, and called him Henchi for short. We enrolled in *hapkido* (martial art) classes. I was too big to fit into any of the uniforms, but *kwan jang nim* (our master) brought in a seamstress to have one custom-made for me, a gesture I greatly appreciated. One day, during the trek to our *dojang* (training space), we encountered a gaggle of schoolchildren, laughing and whipping their miniature backpacks around.

"Annyung!" (Hello!) I greeted them as they met us, testing out my Korean. But instead of bowing or responding, as would be customary for them to do to an elder, they all began screaming, hiding their faces, and running away. That was the first time my heart broke in Korea, and I had to fight back tears as I realized that these kids were frightened of me the same way I was frightened of Frankenstein at their age. I looked like a monster to them.

As it turned out, I didn't fare much better with adults, either. Everywhere I went, people stared at me and made no effort to conceal their reactions to my appearance. There were the passersby who slapped their chests, gasped, and pointed; the shopkeepers who rang up my items and asked, "How many kilograms?"; and a taxi driver who snorted at me for an entire mile.

A few weeks into our stint, a Canadian couple moved into the apartment above ours, and I offered to take the girl, Erin, to go get a pedicure. We slid into a taxi and had begun chatting away when the driver interrupted us. "Hamburger? Pizza? You like?"

Thinking he was just making conversation, we answered, "Oh, yes, delicious," and went back to our conversation, but he continued. "No, no, no! Apples. Orang-ee!" Immediately, it dawned on me that he was trying to give me diet advice, and I didn't want to be humiliated like I was by the last taxi driver, who had made pig noises at me while I sat there powerless, trapped in his backseat.

"Yogiyo," I said. (Stop here, please.) He looked confused, but he took his foot off of the accelerator. *"Yogiyo,"* I repeated, this time more firmly. Finally, he stopped the taxi and pulled over, trying to communicate that we were still several blocks from our destination. *"Gwen-chan-ayo"* (It's okay.) I replied, as I paid him and stepped out. Erin initially looked confused, but had now caught on, and she linked her arm in mine. "I don't mind walking the rest of the way," she said. "I need the exercise anyway."

Having to deal with the rudeness of strangers wasn't easy, to say the least, but I resolved to make the best of it and remain optimistic about the experience. I knew I was the largest person many Koreans had ever seen in real life, and this would naturally provoke a reaction, so I tried to ignore it as best I could. The hours I spent teaching at MoonKkang helped, and I immersed myself into my new job, realizing that I truly loved it. Even though my students spoke mostly beginner English (and low-level intermediate at best), sometimes they hit me with unexpected wisdom. One day I was making conversation with them and asked if they thought North Korea and South Korea should reunite. A student who had never spoken a full sentence in English raised his hand, and with a solemn face, answered, "We have to, Teacher. One family cannot live in two houses."

Not long after that, in the same class, we read an article that detailed the side effects of obesity. The article outlined health problems like high blood pressure, high cholesterol, and diabetes. After we read it aloud, the students turned their papers over, and prepared for the comprehension questions.

"So," I asked, "what is one side effect of obesity?" A quiet, attentive student who went by the name Kerrick raised his hand.

With stone-cold seriousness he answered, "Suicide."

His answer caught me so off guard that I laughed inappropriately. "Well, no . . ." I began. "The article doesn't mention that. I'm obese, right?"

Twelve blank faces looked back at me, nodding.

"Do you think I want to kill myself?"

Kerrick explained, "Teacher, maybe you have some depressions and maybe you want to die."

I shook my head emphatically. "No, I promise you: I do not want to die." I smiled wide. "I'm happy, see?"

That night when I returned home, I couldn't stop thinking about Kerrick's answer. I knew he wasn't being a smart-ass, nor did he mean to be offensive. He genuinely drew the conclusion—not from the article, but from his own experiences—that obesity could lead a person so deep into depression that suicide was the only way out. I knew I wanted to address his reasoning, but I didn't know how to effectively communicate with my students about such a sensitive, complex topic with their limited English. And I wasn't so much stunned by Kerrick's observation as I was saddened that it was the truth. Thousands of geographical miles apart, with more than ten years of an age difference between us—not to mention our respective contrasting cultures and customs—Kerrick and I were both living in societies that caused fat people to consider suicide as an end to their misery. I told myself that, at the very least, I could be an example of a happy fat person and maybe I'd be able to counteract the belief that fat people were all on the verge of killing themselves.

The next day I was teaching a different class, this time in my other classroom located in a corner of the building. Out of the left windows I could see a restaurant named "Beer Girls" in Kon-glish fashion, with the image of two Western schoolgirls and their huge breast implants leering at me. As the students were taking a few minutes to rehearse their report presentations, I heard one boy teasing his classmate.

"You should wear some lipsticks!" he shouted.

"No!" I intervened. "Hey!"

The class quieted down. I asked the student, "Why would you say she needs to wear lipstick?"

"If you are ugly, you wear lipsticks," he replied matter-of-factly.

"No," I said firmly, conveying my seriousness in the tone of my voice. "You do not call people ugly because you think they look different. Do you think I look different? Am I ugly? Is that a nice thing to say? Does that make me happy or sad?"

The student lowered his eyes, as he knew he was being repri-manded. It took me a while to get used to this, as Koreans who are being chastised show respect by not making eye contact.

"Every day in the street people laugh at me," I told them, ex-plaining that people would call me an outsider to my face. "Every day people point at me and say, '*Waegookin!*' [Foreigner!] Every day it makes me sad."

The child who'd been told she needed to wear lipsticks asked me, "Teacher, do you cry?"

"Yes. Sometimes I do."

"Teacher, if *ajumma* (older lady) is looking at you, you should say, '*mianhamnida,*' (I'm sorry.)" she offered.

I smiled at her, to thank her for her advice, but then Scott, one of the smartest students in the class, cleared his throat. He'd been thoughtfully listening to me and I could practically see the wheels turning in his head.

"Teacher, you should not say '*mianhamnida*' because you are not do anything wrong!"

I let out a belly laugh. "Yes, Scott! You are right. You are so smart!" I went over to give him a high-five. Maybe there was progress to be made with these children yet.

Before I knew it a few months had passed and Eric and I used our week of vacation to go to Beijing with some other foreign teachers. We did all the typical sightseeing things, sampled traditional Chinese food, and climbed the Great Wall. When we got back to Daegu, my managers offered me a floating teaching position, which equaled a $100-a-month raise and a lot of extra hassle, as I would be traveling to the different branches (some located in Daegu and some not) to fill in for teachers who were sick or on vacation. Even though it seemed less stable than the position I currently held, I was itching for something new to do and a way to put some space between Eric and me. Because we'd been working together in the same branch and living together for months, our relationship had become tense. Each day when we returned home from work, we ate dinner in silence. He retreated to our small extra room to play computer games and I read or wrote or clicked through the four American channels on our boxy TV until I got sleepy and went to bed alone. Eric and I hadn't had sex in months and I thought the separation during our workday would do each of us some good. I accepted the floating position and readied myself for my first week at a branch roughly thirty minutes away.

It was a muggy, oppressive summer, and I walked several blocks to the subway station. I entered my first classroom hesitantly. The children greeted me with laughter and pointed fingers.

"Teacher. Pig-uh!" one of the students called out. "Teacher. Baby?" another asked, pointing to my stomach. "Teacher is monster!" yet another shouted, laughing hysterically.

When I dragged my weary body up my apartment steps at eleven-thirty that night, I stopped and sat on the stoop. Burying my face in my hands, I heaved a huge sigh. I realized that I'd been able to garner respect from my regular students at my old branch, but each time I walked into a classroom at a different branch, I would have to deal with the same taunts and jeers from a never-ending rotation of new children. How was I going to survive this? I called my mother, who asked me how the first day at my new job went. As much as I wanted to act like I had it all together, I couldn't bullshit her, and the familiar comfort of her voice made me burst into tears. I told her that it was awful; it was a day full of harassment from unruly children.

My stint at this particular branch was to last a week, but I knew that I couldn't tolerate the childish insults that made a mockery of my appearance for four more days. So the next day, when my first group of children entered the classroom, I was ready. Like clockwork, the laughter and uncomfortable whispering ensued. I slammed a book on my desk.

"I'm fat! Okay?" The students looked confused. I went to the board and drew a small eye, with the angular epicanthic fold, and then another that was bigger, with the entire iris visible and long eyelashes that curled upward.

Under the first eye I wrote "Bad." Under the second I wrote "Good."

"Is this true?" I asked them. They looked too scared to move. I softened a little. "It's okay," I said. "Tell me—is this true?" Still nothing. I added more to the small eye: "Korean" and another to the big eye: "American."

"Which one is good? Which one is bad?" I asked. When I put it that way, the students seemed to understand and were remarkably well behaved and respectful for the rest of the class. The next day, the kid who'd called me a pig brought me candy.

Although floating brought new faces, places, and experiences into my daily routine, one thing had not changed: my weight. I'd had the fantasy that moving to a country with a healthier cuisine would melt the pounds off me, but this hadn't happened. I ate far less in Korea than I did in the States, partly because a lot of Western staples weren't available at the neighborhood markets in walking distance of our home. If you wanted bread or cheese, you had to go to the E-Mart (the first-rate Korean equivalent of Walmart), and if you wanted Western snacks, a trip to Costco was in order. It was easiest to eat out, especially at the cheap twenty-four-hour restaurants that were squeezed into each block. Mostly, I ate traditional Korean meals like *jjigae* and *bibimbap,* always with white rice, kimchi, and an array of other small side dishes for a whopping four dollars. Special treats included the sushi place a few blocks down from our apartment, a Subway obscurely tucked into a nearby neighborhood, and a pizza place a few streets over from the branch where Eric still worked.

Since eating a mostly Korean diet had not caused me to drop any weight, I again took matters into my own hands. I went to the grocery store and bought microwaveable rice bowls (one cup each), yogurt, and lots of veggies to eat raw, and then embarked on a near-starvation diet. Each day, I counted my calories, making sure they never totaled more than 1,000. The 300-calorie cup of rice was my favorite part of the day, and I sometimes inhaled it so fast I'd get painful air bubbles in my chest, like the kind that landed me in the emergency room in college. My plan, though unhealthy, was working. I was losing weight. I wrote an email to my dad:

> Today I ate 2 hard-boiled eggs (160/10), a bagel with low fat cheese (240/2), a kiwi (46 /.5), a cup of cherry tomatoes (30 /0), and some tuna (170/.5) for a total of 646 calories and 13 grams of fat. I will probably eat something else because I think under 700 calories is probably too low to be healthy.

My father responded:

I am really getting excited about your diet—maybe this is the time you will make some real progress toward your goal.

At the end of four weeks I had lost twenty pounds, and my pants almost fell off my hips each time I bounded up and down the stairs at work. When you weigh almost 300 pounds, losing twenty doesn't make that much of a visible difference, but Eric could tell. While he was supportive, he campaigned nightly for me to have "just a bite" of the ice cream he was eating, but I steadfastly refused. And I noticed something else in his voice when he commented on my diminishing waistline.

"It's weird to think about you losing weight," he told me. "I feel like everyone will see you how I see you now—that you're perfect."

"You're not afraid I'll leave you, are you?" I teased.

But he answered seriously. "Yes."

I'd taken the floating position, quit the *hapkido* classes, and started going out downtown with Daryl and my other friends without him so that we could have a bit of space, but I still felt restless. I started cherishing my time alone, and we avoided each other in our own apartment. I wrote in my journal (which I hid between my folded sweaters):

Lately I feel so nostalgic about the strangest things. I miss dancing and teaching in sweaty leotards for a minimum of three hours daily. I miss driving around in my Jaguar with Tal and blasting Tori. I miss the mountains. Sometimes, I wait for Eric to leave for hapkido and then I blast my music and dance on my hardwood floor and try to remember old ballet combinations. Sometimes it's such a release that I cry. I've been writing a lot. I've been thinking a lot. I've thought some things that I'm not proud of, but it doesn't stop my mind from spinning in the wrong direction from time to time. If I knew what I was worth, would I be here?

Having fun with my students (2009).

By "here" I didn't mean in Korea—I meant in my relationship. I think both of us knew that it wasn't working out, but neither of us knew how to get out, and maybe we felt more pressure to stay together because we were a million miles away from home.

Eric had scheduled a vacation, alone, to Malaysia, but at the last minute asked me to come along, and I agreed. We fought nearly the entire time we were there. I didn't follow my diet that week, as it was nearly impossible while stuck on a small island called Langkawi, with only a Thai restaurant in walking distance of our hotel. When we returned to Korea, I'd gained almost ten pounds back. I chastised myself for being so weak. Soon after, we reached the end of our first contract and were sent home for a week of vacation.

Coming back to the States, hugging my family, meeting my best friend Heather's newborn daughter, driving my car . . . it was all invigorating and blissful. But, revitalizing as it was, I never thought about not returning to the Land of the Morning Calm, and I even referred to my parents' house as being in "the States" and to Korea as "home." Even though I had only a week to enjoy all the comforts of home, my mother convinced me to go to lunch with my old next-door neighbor, whom I'd grown up calling "Granny Helen." I hadn't seen her in years, and Mom said she wasn't in the best of health and really wanted to get together. We went to one of our favorite restaurants, and as she sat down in the booth across from me, I noticed how much older she looked.

"You've gotten so fat!" she spat. (I also noticed how much more blunt she'd become.) "You should be shot!"

When Eric and I returned to Daegu, we quickly and unceremoniously broke up, divided up our things (I got to keep Henchi, thank God), and moved into new apartments. The breakup that I had been afraid of for years—the pain, the uncertainty, the fear of never being loved again—was far easier than I thought, and it was as if an enormous weight had been lifted off my shoulders. Facing Korea wouldn't be as easy without a partner to fall back on, but I wanted to prove to myself that I could do it.

Meanwhile, there was another change happening on the professional front. I'd floated for a teacher at Young Jae (the "genius" school), and the Korean manager took note of my hard work and enthusiasm and offered me a permanent position. I was beyond thrilled to accept this offer, as most of the students at Young Jae were fluent in English and the curriculum was far more engaging than anything I'd taught before.

My Young Jae students were charming and brilliant, both in academics and in life. In a country where I was so often met with ignorance, these children were an overdue delight and my saving grace. It was my students at Young Jae that made me truly fall in love with Korea, because I fell in love with them. All of them were, without a doubt, smarter than I could ever hope to be, and they constantly surprised me with their detailed understanding of nuanced topics. One day, as I was assigning their homework, I decided to scrap the writing prompt.

"Hmm . . ." I said. "Let's come up with something better."

A student piped up, "Teacher, how about differing opinions on transgenders and where they should use the bathroom to feel safe."

I nearly fell out of my chair. For growing up in a culture that staunchly believes in fan death (the belief that sleeping in a closed room with a running fan can kill you by sucking the oxygen out of the room—I'm not kidding; all of the fans have self-timers to save you from certain death), my students were forward-thinking as hell, and I felt privileged to be their teacher. They were empathetic, too. Once, when a student sensed I was having a bad day, he gave me his cloth pencil case with cats on it, simply because he knew I liked it.

While I was busy enjoying my new freedom from a long-term relationship, and focusing on a new job, I was surprised to find that Eric settled easily into the role of my friend. We stayed in touch, he hung up framed paintings in my fifth-floor walkup, and I babysat his new cat when he went out of town. It was an unlikely turn of events, but it was a welcome one. We even decided to take a trip to Vietnam with Daryl and his boyfriend, Tyler, just the four of us.

I have major wanderlust, and visiting any new place is a thrilling adventure for me, but unfortunately this vacation wasn't the kind of relaxing break I was craving. Just walking the streets in Vietnam can make you feel vulnerable; there is the typical exaggerated reaction at seeing a fat foreigner, but coupled with this is persistent barking from street vendors who swear they have "big size!" Of course, they didn't have a size big enough for *me,* so I was pumped to hear that tailors in Hoi An (our first vacation stop) were a big draw. The boys got measured for knock-off North Face jackets and three-piece suits. I, on the other hand, just wanted five or so cotton T-shirts in different colors, customized to fit my body perfectly. The seamstresses furrowed their brows when they measured me and guffawed at having to fasten two measuring tapes together to fit my hips. I was too used to this behavior to be anything other than mildly annoyed by it, but when the seamstresses quoted me a price equivalent to that of Daryl's three-piece suit, I was vexed. I rubbed the thin cotton material of my shirt between my fingers and tried to barter in simple English, but got nowhere.

"So much fabric!" she shot back, shrugging.

I was indignant and refused to buy anything, stalking back down the block to our hotel, seething under the Vietnamese sun. I sat on our first-level patio overlooking the pool and waited for the boys to get back. A girl who had been swimming emerged from the water and walked toward me, taking a seat in the empty chair beside me. I found this odd, considering she was on my private patio, but gave her an awkward smile. Her eyes darted back and forth. Something was so off about her. Saying she made me uneasy would be a gross understatement.

Out of nowhere, she stared at me intensely and said, in a Scottish accent, "You're so fat. You're gonna have a heart attack. You're gonna die."

"Please leave," I said. She glared at me and didn't budge. I went inside my room and locked the door, then reported her behavior to the front desk. The clerk said they'd been having various problems with her throughout her stay, and I couldn't shake the bizarre vibe she gave off. Later that night, Daryl, Tyler, Eric, and I were swimming when she appeared poolside holding a large rock from the stone arrangements in the grass. She hurled it at my head and it landed in the water in front of me with a loud plunk.

Soon, my parents made the trip to Korea for a visit. For the past couple of years I had been telling them about the harassment I suffered on a daily basis, but when they got there, nothing out of the ordinary seemed to happen. It even occurred to me that they might think I had embellished the stories of people laughing and snorting at me. I took them to the usual spots in my neighborhood, and even invited them to sit in on my classes at Young Jae. After the first day, my mother hugged me close with tears in her eyes.

"I'm so sorry," she whispered into my ear.

"For what?" I asked.

"For how awful everyone is to you."

Confused, I asked her what she was talking about. She and my father described the looks and snickers that had been trailing us all day. I hadn't even noticed anyone looking at me at all. I'd become immune to the things that shocked my parents.

Just behind my apartment building there was a Jeep dealership, and one day my dad found himself striking up a conversation with the owner. Naturally, my dad spoke no Korean and the man spoke little English, but my dad communicated to him that his daughter lived in the apartments behind the dealership and that he was visiting from America. The owner told my dad that he knew me (presumably from seeing me come and go) and gestured wildly with his arms outstretched, evoking an image of my size. "Always eating!" he said to my father, miming shoving food in his face. My dad didn't tell me that story until months after I'd moved home, but it bothered him to his core.

The day after my parents left to go back to North Carolina, I was walking the half mile to work when a well-dressed man in his thirties swerved dangerously close to me on his bicycle.

"Pig-uh!" He sneered and spit at me. He missed, but I was enraged and ran after him (a futile attempt for me, especially because he was on a bike) and screamed the Korean equivalent of "motherfucker" at him until my voice was hoarse and he had disappeared.

A couple weeks later, on that same street, I was confronted with the worst thing that ever happened to me while I was in Korea.

There was an establishment called Hof 'N' Joy that served beer and liquor and some appetizer type dishes, and we often went there after work to relax. This particular night, my friends and I shared a long table with some Korean teachers from our branch. I was seated in between my friends Daryl and Ian. Toward the back of the restaurant there was a drunk Korean man sitting with two friends who kept complaining that the flash from pictures we were taking was hurting his eyes. He got into a heated argument with our female Korean friend and eventually the owner told him he had to leave. As he left with his friends, he locked eyes with me, and I didn't lower my gaze. He muttered something in Korean. I was seated with my back to the door just a few feet away when he suddenly burst back inside and started punching me in the head. Before I could even think, I was on my feet as Daryl and Ian wrestled him to the floor. I'd never been in a physical altercation before, and adrenaline was surging through me. I screamed at him in English and one of the guys told the owner to call the police.

Within moments, the police arrived and the man retreated to his knees in a full and complete bow, repeating *"Mianhamnida"* (I'm sorry) over and over. I told him to go fuck himself and went to the police station to file a report. The next week, a friend brought me to a bigger police station to give my official state-ment with a government translator. At work, my manager pulled me aside and revealed that the man had contacted her to apolo-gize. She asked if I would consider dropping the charges against him because he could lose his career and reputation. I told her no, that I wanted to handle this the same way I would if it had happened in the States. She pressed me further, pointing out that he was drunk and stressed-out.

"Then he needs to learn not to assault unsuspecting foreign women," I told her. Later, I was told that if we went to court, my case would most certainly be dropped, he would suffer no repercussions, and that would be that. But if I agreed to drop the charges, he would pay me 300,000 won, roughly the equivalent of $300. After speaking with several Koreans I trusted, who all echoed the same sentiment, I figured it was better for him to suffer the consequence of having to pay me money rather than nothing at all, so I took his money.

It was the beginning of my third year in Daegu, and I was offered yet another promotion, which I accepted. My new job was in the editing department, where I would work with the foreign and Korean teams developing and editing curriculum. The editing department operated on a different schedule than teaching, from nine in the morning to six at night, instead of four-thirty to ten-thirty P.M. Because of this, I started to lose touch with some of my friends, missing the post-work outings I'd come to enjoy so much. I began a nightly ritual of leaving work, stopping by the corner store to buy six tall boys, and going home to drink alone. I felt lonely and worn down by the constant torment. I spent my nights drunk in my apartment with Henchi, chatting on the computer with my friends Heather and Ashley from home. It was time to evaluate where I was in my life and where I wanted to go. I had a successful career in Korea. I was respected by my students, coworkers, and superiors. I'd traveled to China, Malaysia, Vietnam, Japan, and Indonesia. I'd saved thousands of dollars. Why was I so miserable? As my father wrote to me in an email:

You are not giving yourself the credit you deserve. You have accomplished a lot, but you want to accomplish so much more which is what has got you second-guessing yourself. Look at what is important to you and start working on those things.

As I thought about my passions, three things stuck out to me: dance, psychology (my minor in college), and helping others.

"I wish there was, like ... dance therapy," I told my friend Heather.

Heather responded with a link from Google. Apparently, dance therapy *was* a thing. I immediately filled out applications for the few graduate programs in the country that offered it. She also told me that her husband, Jared, was working out with a local trainer in Greensboro and successfully losing weight. I

With my friend Jeonghui. I weighed 280 pounds (2009).

knew that I wanted to make some big changes in my life and would need a plan in place for whenever I decided to leave Korea, so I jotted down the trainer's name for safekeeping. Around this time, the Jeep dealership behind my apartment closed down and the building was renovated into a Burger King. For the foreigners in my neighborhood, this was a pretty big deal, as Western food wasn't the easiest thing to come by. (Several of us had even taken a special trip to Seoul to wait in line for forty minutes when a Taco Bell opened—something, as a fat woman, I never would have done if I didn't have ten skinny friends who begged me to go along.) Having a Burger King so close by was tempting; late at night, the smell of cheeseburgers and French fries wafted through my open bedroom window, and finally, after it had been open for a week, I gave myself a "fat-girls-are-allowed-to-be-seen-in-fast-food-restaurants" pep talk and sailed through the double doors ready to satisfy my grumbling stomach. Just in front of the counter there were several guys milling about and I asked in English, "Are you in line?" I immediately wondered why I had done that, as I never approached a Korean in English first, but one of the guys responded in perfect English, "No, no. You go ahead."

I was taken aback because, in my experience, even Koreans who know English well are hesitant to use it outside of the classroom. "Thank you," I said as I stepped forward. The guy took a step forward, too. He asked me my name, told me I had beautiful eyes, and then asked for my phone number. Certain that he was looking for an English lesson, I gave it to him, got my food, and left without giving it another thought, until the guy, Ji-hoon, texted me and asked me on a date.

I learned through texting that Ji-hoon had lived abroad in Australia for a few years. Now, at twenty-seven, he was a university student studying to be an engineer. Ji-hoon came on so strong in the beginning that I was slightly turned off, but he was determined and tireless in his quest to date me. He sent me text messages relentlessly, each one beginning with a different pet name. He had crowned me his "Burger Queen," a tribute, of course, to where we met, but his creativity didn't stop there. One day I was his "round, robust darling" and the next he called me his "plump princess." When he called me his "elliptical goddess" he admitted that he'd run out of synonyms for "curvy" and had consulted the thesaurus. So when I finally invited Ji-hoon to my apartment, I asked him why he was so interested in me. It's no secret that fat women don't fit into the Korean beauty standard, and I'd thought a Korean man finding me physically attractive was next to impossible.

"I have a fat brother," Ji-hoon explained, running his hands through my hair. "So I was conditioned at an early age to get used to fat people. And you are so beautiful; you're like a super-model."

Ji-hoon and I got along well. He shared my sense of humor and we laughed a lot. For the first time in all my years in Korea, I had an intimate partner who could help me do things that had always been difficult. And in retrospect, it was no coincidence that I met him at a fast-food joint—Ji-hoon loved to eat. In fact, Ji-hoon, as tiny as he was, ate more than any human being I'd ever known before or since. He noted that quantity of food was more important than quality, and he routinely ordered an appetizer, two meals, and a dessert all to himself. When that settled an hour later, he'd pop off the couch and ask, "Ice cream?" before hurrying off to the corner store and returning with the ice cream, chips, and candy, which he'd finish off before bed. As much as I wondered if his eating habits were "normal," I was, in a sense, grateful for them. When I was with Ji-hoon, I never worried that he would think I was a pig if I ate five pieces of pizza instead of two. I never had to make myself uncomfortable by asking for food at all, because Ji-hoon had it covered. Even on days when he wasn't with me, he'd call for sushi or Korean or Italian to be delivered to my apartment. Until I started dating

Ji-hoon, food delivery was a luxury I never got to enjoy because of the language barrier, but now I was discovering all kinds of delicious food, Korean and otherwise, that I hadn't had easy access to while I was in Korea. Feeding someone is an act of love, and it was only one of the ways he sought to take care of me. A couple of months into our relationship, I could feel my clothes getting tighter. I wasn't sure if Ji-hoon noticed; he always remarked about how I was perfect, but he'd wag his finger at me and say, "But no bigger, okay?"

I wasn't sure if I really loved Ji-hoon, but he was a Band-Aid on the wounds that Korea had inflicted on me. When we went out in public, he proudly held my hand and showed me physical affection in spite of all the people who looked at us like we were circus freaks. One night when we were out at a club, a drunk American military guy sidled up next to me and asked me to teach him how to dance. I knew by the glances he kept throwing to his friends and his tone of voice that he was making fun of me. Ji-hoon knew it, too, and he took a swing at the guy (and got us kicked out). Another night, while we were having drinks with friends, a group of girls asked if they could take my picture, and when I politely declined, they kept trying to covertly snap photos of me while laughing and talking in Korean about how fat I was. Ji-hoon marched over and knocked an expensive Canon camera right out of the hands of one of the girls. But his protective, aggressive streak wasn't always directed outward—he'd begun turning on me, becoming irrationally jealous and controlling. He constantly accused me of cheating on him; he broke my furniture in fits of rage; he stalked me outside of my apartment when he should have been in class. After several months, I'd finally had enough of his possessiveness and hair-trigger temper, and I broke up with him. He left me twenty-seven voicemails, tried to force his way into my apartment, and stood beneath my window shouting that I was a whore.

The next six months in Korea were darkened by the familiar

shadow of depression. I went to work, came home to my apartment, and drank alone until I was numb. On weekends, I sometimes stayed in bed all day, while Henchi sat nestled on the windowsill or on my pillow, refusing to leave the bedroom until I did. During one phone conversation with my mom, as I tried to describe the futility I felt, I told her that as long as I was in Korea, I didn't think I could ever be happy. It had been years and I was sure I was as culturally assimilated as I could ever hope to be, but I couldn't handle the way my body felt like a target. My mom reminded me of all the wonderful qualities I possessed and urged me to stay positive. But even then, I told her, it wouldn't change the way *other* people saw me. In the end it didn't really matter how awesome, worthwhile, or beautiful I thought I was if no one else could recognize it. I rationalized that even the most genuinely happy person in the world couldn't survive in a place that didn't want them. Growing up as a privileged white girl, I'd never experienced such a resounding sense of "otherness" that could incite disdain and even abuse.

I debated whether I wanted to stay in Korea. I loved making money and traveling, but I'd also unexpectedly secured an audition with the dance therapy department at the renowned Pratt Institute. I was positive I wouldn't get in, though, and I didn't want to be stuck in the States with no job prospects. One minute, the thought of leaving Korea seemed scary, but in the next it seemed like the obvious answer to my problems.

On the street, I was used to taunts and jeers, gross disrespect, prying questions about my weight and body, and now even violence, but I'd also made some wonderful friends. One of them, named Narae, made it her mission in life to make me comfortable in her country. She made and brought me breakfast every day, even though I begged her not to.

Narae's mother prepared traditional Korean meals to give to me on holidays because I was spending them alone. Occasionally, a stranger would do something so kind it would blow my mind, like the time I stood at the crosswalk getting drenched in a downpour and a young, beautiful woman pressed her open umbrella into my hand, wrapping my fingers around the handle before she flitted off in her high heels, protecting her head from the rain with only her hands.

Despite these acts of kindness, the streets still felt like a war zone. There was a particular group of men who'd taken to harassing me daily at the crosswalk on my way to work. They worked at an auto body store, and each day, as I was waiting for the light to change, they would yell and gesture at me. One day, when I'd had enough, I turned around and yelled, "What are you looking at?" in Korean.

This angered them, and they stepped off their property, getting in my face, yelling "Fuck you!" at me. When I arrived at work, I relayed the story to a Korean friend who was so horrified that she told one of our managers, who called the auto body store and let the boss know what his employees were doing to me. They were fired on the spot. Having my manager stand up for me in this way was both incredibly touching and unexpected, but the incident pushed me over the edge.

My contract was up for renewal the next month, and I found myself sitting alone, making pro and con lists to try to figure out my next step. As I looked back on the last few years, I realized I'd accomplished a significant number of things, and I hadn't jumped on a plane back to the States when the going got tough, like some ESL teachers did. I'd survived a breakup, discrimination, harassment, and even physical abuse—and I'd thrived, working my way up the entire MoonKkang system. I hadn't lost all my hope or optimism, but all of the difficult encounters had begun to sap my spirit, and that frightened me. I knew one thing for sure: if I went home, I would commit myself to losing weight. Korea was my first experience with overt bigotry due to my weight, and it sparked in me an indignation I'd never felt before. Surely, I hadn't deserved to be treated like *this,* but the only thing I could think of that would guarantee that I wouldn't be treated like this again was losing weight. I packed my life back up into suitcases, took Henchi, and boarded a plane back home, determined to fix my problems—to fix my body— once and for all.

7

LOSING 100 POUNDS
DIDN'T MAKE ME HAPPY

The morning of January 17, 2011, was gray and rainy. My dad's voice, brimming with excitement, woke me with a start.

"Let's get goin', girl!"

Having gotten only a couple hours of sleep, I rolled over away from my dad and buried my head under the pillow. He snatched it away immediately.

"C'mon, girl! This is the first day of the rest of your life!"

I could think of at least a hundred things I'd rather spend the first day of the rest of my life doing than waking up at the crack of dawn to go meet my new trainer, Will, but by this time my dad had drawn the blinds and flooded my cocoon with light. I peeled myself out of bed slowly, jiggling my limbs to shake the lethargy off.

As I drove to No Gear Fitness, I zeroed in on the rhythmic squeaky sound of my windshield wipers and willed myself not to cry. Besides sleep deprivation, I was wrestling with fear of failure, performance anxiety, and the uncomfortable sensation of being stuffed into a pair of two-sizes-too-small Lycra athletic

The day I started training with Will, 329 pounds (2011).

pants from Walmart. There was so much riding on the next hour, and I couldn't recall a time in recent memory when one singular event had held so much power over the course of my life. I'd told myself, in no uncertain terms, that if I couldn't accomplish my goal this time, I would have to resign myself to being fat forever, and I couldn't bear to think about a life like that. This was the day I would start over, and from here on out, no mistakes could be made. This was the fresh start, the redo, the clean slate, the *last* chance—and the self-imposed finality of it was petrifying.

A few minutes later I cautiously inched my way inside the gym. The old sweat smell, the humid air, and the clanging of machines seemed simultaneously foreign and familiar, and I felt wildly out of place. Will was physically intimidating, the kind of guy who might make your palms sweat if he looked at you the wrong way, but his eyes were soft and he had a friendly smile. The first thing he wanted to evaluate was how long it would take me to walk a mile on the treadmill. I glanced nervously at the clock. "What if I can't finish in time?" He laughed at my question, but I didn't crack a smile in return. I was genuinely worried that it might take our entire fifty-minute session for me to walk a mile, but I stepped onto the treadmill anyway. After five minutes I felt like I was done for. After five more I felt some electricity in my legs, so I picked up the pace a little bit. Pretty soon I was doing some semblance of jogging, and when the red lights on the treadmill read *1.00,* only eighteen minutes had elapsed. Nowhere near as bad as I thought.

Will led me to the back room, where we did what he called "dynamic warm-ups"—high knees, Russian walks, under-the-fence-over-the-fence. Then, I ducked underneath a rope and punched on either side. The exercises were easier to execute than I'd thought they'd be, but when our time was up and we walked to the front of the gym to weigh in, my legs hit Jell-O status.

"I'm going to put you on a ten-day detox," he announced as I stepped on the scale. "Three hundred and twenty-nine."

Three hundred and twenty-nine? My jaw was on the floor. The last time I had weighed myself in Korea I was 280-something. I'd been able to maintain a weight of approximately 280 pounds for the last two years of college and the first two years of Korea, and now I was *forty-nine* pounds heavier? I knew I had gained weight from all the social dinners and snacks with Ji-hoon; my clothes had gotten tighter over the months we'd dated, but they'd all still fit. I estimated that I'd gained ten pounds or so, but here I was, having gained practically fifty pounds without realizing it. The shameful number flashed on the scale like emergency blinkers.

Will, oblivious to my devastation, penciled in the number on a paper in his file folder and then handed me a couple of loose-leaf sheets with meal plans and a grocery list. "See you Wednesday," he said.

I was so physically worn-down and emotionally drained that I skipped the grocery store, telling myself I'd go the next day. When I got home, I headed straight for the warm protection of the couch and sent myself out of the real world and back into sleep. Later that evening when I woke up, I went to Heather's house to tell her about how the session had gone. Her husband, Jared, had trained with Will that day, too, but his session was after mine.

"Will said you did really good for a first session," Jared told me. My inner child who always needs a gold star swelled with pride.

"I'm not even that sore," I bragged.

"You will be. The day after I started, I couldn't even lift Ava out of her crib."

The next morning Jared's prediction came to fruition. I could barely lift myself out of bed, let alone tend to an infant. I had never, in all my years of physical activity, felt anything close to the excruciating pain that permeated every bone, muscle, and tendon of my body. My core was so fatigued that I could barely sit up. I couldn't lower myself onto the toilet. Instead I grabbed the towel rack, aimed, and fell. I thought back over the amount of formal exercise I'd done over the last ten years. Sure, I'd walked to and from work and around my neighborhood every day in Korea, but even a night out of vigorous dancing used to make me stiff. The mornings following such an evening were a nightmare, especially for my feet. The arches would tense up and the balls were so sensitive that just getting to my bathroom in my bare feet required me to hang on to furniture to help lessen the pain. Now my muscles felt like they were on the verge of a total and complete shutdown.

I lumbered down the stairs, slowly and yelping in pain, and climbed into my car to go to the grocery store. As I leaned on my cart for support, taking small, shuffling steps through the aisles, I wondered if I could even make it through my entire list. I tossed broccoli and lettuce into the cart. Then chicken breasts, turkey bacon, apples, and something called apple cider vinegar. By the time I got home I could only muster enough energy to throw the food in the fridge and collapse back onto the couch.

The next morning the soreness was even worse. My mom heard me squealing and called downstairs: "Whitney! You can't go anywhere like that. Just call him and tell him you're hurt. This is ridiculous."

"No!" I yelled back, cursing myself for somehow getting this out of shape. "I can't not show up the second day."

When I arrived at Will's gym, after savoring every second of near-motionlessness in my car (aside from the pain that shot through my calf every time I pushed the brake), I gingerly lowered myself onto the couch just inside the door and waited for him to finish up with another client. When he was done, he strode toward me smiling.

"Honestly," I said, "I'm not a wuss, but . . ."

"You're sore?"

"Yes. So bad that I just really don't think I can even . . ."

Will stared at me, no hint of sympathy on his face. "You made it to the couch, didn't you? If you can walk in that door, you can train. C'mon."

I hobbled behind him, struggling to keep up. But he was right. I could train. Once we got about twenty minutes in, my aching muscles started to loosen up some, and somehow I got through an entire second session without losing consciousness or dying right there on the floor.

After my third session with Will on that Friday, my friend Ashley, who had basically moved into our extra room downstairs, and I decided to go see *Black Swan*. My muscles were really tender and I had a hard time going up the barely raised theatre steps.

"Everyone's looking at me like, 'Daaaamn, that fat bitch can't even walk!' They don't know I'm sore from working out!" I joked. I'd been eating by-the-book clean for four days now.

- Breakfasts of a hard-boiled egg and piece of turkey bacon.
- Then, a workout.
- Next, a drive-through Starbucks for a venti iced coffee with skim milk and two Splendas.
- Go home.
- Eat an apple and a handful of nuts. Sleep on the couch. Make a salad with blueberries for lunch. Late afternoon, eat an apple and two ounces of cheese.
- Watch TV.
- Waddle to the kitchen one more time around seven P.M. for two ounces of chicken and a cup of broccoli. Sleep. Repeat.

I didn't dare dream of messing up my diet this early, so I wrapped my arms inside my jacket and settled in for the movie.

I thought about plugging up my nostrils and mouth-breathing for the duration of the film just to avoid the popcorn aroma. The movie transfixed me. I watched the dancers and remembered what it was like to sweat from every pore, to be lean, to feel pressure, to perform, and to succeed. Maybe, I thought, just maybe, I'm on my way back there.

By day ten of my detox there was good news and bad news. The good: I'd lost ten pounds. The bad: I had to leave abruptly that day to drive my mom down to Mississippi to tend to some family business for a week. I hadn't had my license renewed since I'd been home back in the States, so I'd have to go to the DMV for that, too. Will gave me instructions to follow my diet the best I could, to try to walk at least three times, and on Friday, I could have my first cheat day—an entire day of unrestricted eating. I left the gym for the DMV and when it came my turn, still dressed in my tank top and hoodie, my sweaty hair pulled back, I realized that for the first time in quite a while it wasn't hard to smile. I felt happy. When I got back in the car, I opened up Facebook. I didn't update my status very often, as I felt I didn't have much to say, and never wanted to be someone who recorded every mundane detail of her life. I wonder if I should say anything, I thought. I didn't want to jinx myself. Eh, fuck it. *Day 10 = 10 pounds lost.* Post.

When I got home my dad helped me load up the car with my scale, my George Foreman grill, various Mrs. Dash seasonings, and measuring cups. I kept a cooler of food in the front seat with my mom for the twelve-hour drive. I promised my dad I would keep to my plan, and I did. Every four hours on the road, I pulled over to gobble down my small meal or snack. During the week, I walked through the neighborhood, almost finishing a mile. I said no to every diet drink, sweet tea, or piece of gum that was offered to me. By the end of the week I'd lost another three pounds. I was elated and ready for my cheat day. The next morning I headed out of my uncle's house to McDonald's, where I indulged in not one, but two of my favorite sausage, egg, and cheese biscuits and I gulped down a large sweet tea. Later that evening I had a pasta dish when we went out to eat. This isn't so bad, I reasoned. Go through hell for six days and eat on the seventh. Doable. When I woke up the next morning, I hopped on the scale to see the damage. I was dumbfounded. The scale said my cheat day had resulted in an additional ten pounds. That was every bit of weight I'd just lost. I called Will in a panic.

"That's okay," he said. "Get back on the plan. Come see me Monday."

Over the weekend, I managed to lose only a couple of the pounds I'd gained on my cheat day. Will talked to me about water retention but seemed surprised at my misfortune. He explained that most people gained two or three pounds of water weight after a day of unrestricted eating. But I had gained ten. This experience would foreshadow the rest of my weight-loss venture. It was an endless cycle, even when I ate one cheat meal, and a fairly sensible one at that. Anything that I didn't make in my own kitchen from scratch, including the "Under 550 Calories" meals at Applebee's, caused me to bloat and swell in my fingers and toes. On Saturdays I weighed in at least five, sometimes seven or eight, pounds heavier. I'd hit the gym, intermittently jumping on the scale to see if I'd lost anything. When I was done working out, I usually noticed my dark shirts encrusted with a curious white stain, but it happened only on Saturdays. One day I had a lightbulb moment: it was the salt from my Friday cheat meals drying in my sweat.

One Friday, Ashley and I tried an experiment. We'd spent the afternoon sitting in my car, sipping sugary Starbucks coffees and talking. We decided to have lunch at Arby's and ordered the same meal in the same size. When we got home we both weighed ourselves again, after having both done so that morning. Ashley's weight had fluctuated three-tenths of a pound. Mine had gone up four pounds. How was this possible? What was wrong with my body? I tried to voice my frustrations to Will, but he assured me that if I stuck to the plan, I would see success. He asked me to trust him, and I did.

On March 10, when I came home from Will's on Friday morning, my parents were packing for a weekend trip. I told them the news: I'd lost thirty pounds in fifty-three days. My dad wrote me a check for $300 to celebrate the event. I recorded the milestone in a notebook I'd been keeping of my daily weights, exercise, and achievements.

"Let's go get matching tattoos to commemorate this," Tal suggested to Ashley and me that night, tickling my impulsive streak. A half hour later the three of us were staring at the wall of a tattoo shop downtown.

"What should we get?" I asked, flipping through laminated pages of hearts, stars, and skulls. "What's the most important thing we have in common?"

Tal spotted a minuscule, ambiguous wing that could also pass for a leaf or a feather. Small was a requirement because I wasn't ready to tattoo any parts of my body that would be drastically diminishing in size.

"I like it! We should put them on our ankles. And it'll remind me that my feet can take me anywhere." I didn't realize until it was all said and done that our ankles would perfectly resemble the Goodyear tire logo, but you win some and you lose some, right? To this day, every few months or so, either Tal or I text each other: *Is our tattoo a wing or a feather?* and the other will respond: *A wing.* Five minutes later: *I think.*

The decision to tattoo something permanently on my body that I associated with weight loss was a turning point of epic proportions. Prior to that day, I was worried that my weight loss was just a phase, kind of like the two-week period in elementary school when I answered only to the name Sasha, or when I discovered Ani DiFranco in college and grappled for a whole month with the feeling that I was, and had probably always been, a lesbian. But now I knew my weight-loss kick wasn't going to pass. In the nine years since I'd first started gaining weight, I'd never once managed to lose more than twenty pounds. Losing thirty made it feel *real*.

Galvanized by this breakthrough, I ramped up my exercise even more. On Mondays and Wednesdays I trained with Will in the morning, then went home for coffee (by this time, I was taking it black) and a nap (because I'm logical like that). When I woke up, it was back to the gym for another workout—maybe twenty minutes on the hardest level of the StairMaster or an hour-long date with the treadmill. I could now jog three miles without stopping and I felt invincible. On Tuesdays and Thursdays, I spent the mornings dragging my mom to the YMCA where, much to her chagrin, I'd purchased her a senior membership. On those nights, I attended Will's boot camp classes where I shone as the biggest but most devoted person in the group. On Fridays, I attended my regular session with Will and then took the rest of the day off. Saturdays and Sundays I was back at it with swimming, playing soccer with my dad, or running the steps at the local high school. This strenuous regimen was made possible by the fact that I was living at home with my parents who actively discouraged me from getting a job in favor of concentrating 100 percent of my attention on losing weight. And losing weight had become the only meaningful thing in my life. With no job and few friends, the only triumphs or disappointments I experienced were hitched to three glowing digits. I had no boyfriend or boss; my avid allegiance knew only one master: the scale.

My goal was to lose fifty pounds in ninety days, which happened to fall directly on my birthday. After ninety days I'd made it to 48 pounds lost, so I'd have to wait to celebrate that milestone. I'd made Will promise me that he would perform the

Cupid Shuffle (I'm really dating myself here) and let me film it when I hit minus fifty pounds.

I was satisfied with losing 48 pounds by my birthday. It was a Thursday night (i.e., not my cheat day), so I waited until the next night to celebrate. Heather, Tal, Todd, Ashley, and a few other friends met me for hibachi. I was excited about being able to eat it. We enjoyed a delicious meal and returned to my parents' house. As per tradition, Heather bought me an ice cream cake and my dad made a toast before we dug in. He'd been in his robe, sipping merlot for at least two hours, and he spoke about my achievements and how proud he was of me, clapping me on the back and hugging me. I was so happy to make him proud that I forgave him when he kept butting his head into the playroom to say "just one more thing" and continue boasting about me.

The next morning I had gained eleven pounds from the celebration, but I was so close to the fifty-pound mark and I would not be denied. I worked myself to the bone for two days, hopping on and off the scale after each mile I ran that weekend. On Monday morning I still had three more pounds of water weight to lose. I headed to the Y at six-thirty and ran some more. By 9:55, when I was finished with my workout with Will, all eleven pounds of water weight had disappeared, and by the middle of the week I hit my fifty-pound goal. I bought iron-on letters from a craft store and made T-shirts for Will and myself that proclaimed *Club 50* on the front. On the back, Will's read, *Will: Beast Mode Since Birth.* Mine read, *Whitney: Beast Mode Since January.*

Losing weight became my singular obsession. I'd started eating less than my 1,100-calorie diet called for, consuming only just enough to get by. I replaced my cheat day sausage, egg, and cheese biscuit with a homemade sandwich of wheat bread, a scrambled egg, two pieces of real bacon, and a slice of American cheese. I compulsively weighed myself every time I walked by the scale, even running downstairs in the middle of the night if I'd woken up, like an impatient child waiting to see if Santa had come. I took all my PCOS medications, a routine that had previously eluded me. I sobbed uncontrollably when one Friday I discovered my dad had eaten the ice cream I'd purchased for my cheat meal before I had a bite. I dreamed about food that never touched my lips. I got off on outperforming boot camp class members half my size. I relished when strangers in whatever gym I happened to be in came up to me out of the blue to tell me how impressed they were.

One Monday morning in the gym, I broke down with Will. I hadn't lost my cheat day weight yet. He asked me why I was so upset.

The day I hit my fifty-pound goal (2011).

"Because," I blurted, "I've been throwing up everything I eat on Fridays!" His demeanor turned very serious. "Whitney," he said sternly, holding my gaze with his, "you gotta get all this crazy shit outta your head!" I'd never heard Will curse before, so I knew he meant business. And I knew he was right, but I didn't know how to do it. It didn't seem fair. I'd heard about other people my size dropping a hundred pounds by cutting out soda and walking a mile every day. Yes, I lost weight every week, sometimes one-and-a-half pounds and sometimes six, but I had to work my ass off for it. I was killing myself and felt like I had zero margin for error.

On Friday mornings after my session and weigh-in with Will, I'd call my father with a report, and I was feeling increasingly obsessed with my progress. My dad took more pride in me than I did. He was the one who talked me off a thousand different ledges, day or night. He was the one who prepared me a nightly foot bath of ice water and Epsom salts to ease the pain in my feet. He was the one who would be by my bedside at seven-thirty to spoon-feed me plain Greek yogurt with agave syrup while I lay in bed, begging for one more hour of sleep. My dad was my coach, not my enemy. I knew this to be true—so why was I so afraid of disappointing him? Could it be that he had told me this was the single most exciting time in his life, after marrying my mother, my brother's birth and my own? It was no secret that my dad was living through me, floating through bad days at work on the memory of how much weight I'd lost that week. And I knew that it was something he'd always wanted for me, not only for my health, but because he knew it would make me happy.

He knew that if I lost weight, I would get my due. I wouldn't have to deal with asshole boyfriends and prying eyes and nasty judgments. I'd have my pick of men who deserved me. I could stop watching my old dance videos and actually perform the routines instead. I could live up to my potential. He told me time and time again that he was amazed by me.

"You," he'd say, "are doing the hardest thing in the world. You could be a lawyer, or a doctor, and it wouldn't be half as hard. What I see you do day in and day out, the iron will it takes—the work ethic it takes, the sheer determination it takes—there's only one percent of people in the entire world who can do what you're doing."

The following months boasted a slew of accomplishments. *May 6: 59 pounds lost. May 27: 67 pounds lost.* I called Todd and told him I was ready to dance.

"Bring the choreo. Something I can do," I said. Todd brought Adele and some beautiful choreography to go with it. Just like old times, we slid the furniture to the perimeter of the room and used our reflection in the TV as a mirror. We danced for hours until we were ready to film it.

In the beginning of the video, Todd introduces us: "This is Todd and Whitney, 2011. Carrying the dream. Decades strong . . ."

Watching this video now gives me chills, as I'm watching the beginning of Fat Girl Dancing, even though we didn't call it that at the time. Who could have ever imagined where our dream would carry us? I posted the video on my Facebook page, for all of my nine hundred friends to see.

By June, I'd lost 8.5 inches from my hips, seven from my waist, three from my thighs, and 2.5 from my biceps. I was really slimming down, and I fantasized about taking some kind of dance class. One of my friends had mentioned an adult beginner's ballet class offered in the City Arts building—the same place I used to rehearse for community theatre shows as a teenager. We decided to go.

When we entered the class, I couldn't believe what I was doing. It took a lot of balls for a self-proclaimed dancer to attend a class in the style of dance she was worst at performing. My last ballet class had been nine years ago. I feigned stretching, inhaling and exhaling slowly, waiting for the teacher to arrive. And when she did, I was so relieved. Ms. Garen was approximately 106 years old (okay, I later found out she was actually ninety-three), with leathery skin and an orthopedic boot on her ankle. As she made her way to the front of the room, I whispered a thank-you to the universe. I was going to be okay.

But the universe had other plans that day, and Ms. Garen, in all of her geriatric glory, was no joke. Before we even left the barre, I was covered in sweat, suffering cramps in muscles I didn't remember I had. As we completed some basic positions, Ms. Garen met my gaze. I looked away in fear, of course.

"This is not your first ballet class." It should have been a question, but she stated it.

"Yes. No. It's not. Ma'am."

When we broke to go across the floor, I took a deep breath and tried my best, despite barely being able to whip my body around in one full revolution. Don't even make me talk about the spotting situation or the grande jeté. As I haphazardly bounded toward the opposite corner, Ms. Garen stood next to my friend, resting on her cane.

"It's really such a shame," she said, gesturing toward me. "She would be a great dancer if she weren't so fat."

My notebook continued to fill up with numbers, measurements, and sentiments. *July 15: 80 pounds lost. Three-week plateau is over. Lowest weight in 7 years!! Only twenty more pounds until I lose one-half of my goal weight!*

However, I was beginning to feel restless, and I craved something more to look forward to every day than hard-boiled eggs and beating my circuit times. I'd convinced my dad that I needed to work, but he disagreed. He thought working would cause me to lose sight of my weight-loss goals, but I told him I was going crazy. I applied for several copy-editor jobs but didn't hear anything back, so I headed to retail. Target hired me on the spot.

Now that I had a job, I realized that sporting the red and khaki for minimum wage wasn't really fulfilling me, either. Something else was missing.

On a whim, I joined OkCupid. I'd heard that online dating wasn't "weird" anymore, and I had no life outside of the gym and Target. I wasn't sure I was ready to go back to ballet, but I'd heard of something called Zumba. They offered a class at the Y, so I looked up the class schedule and made plans to attend.

When I got to Zumba, I claimed a spot in the front row. I knew this would make me vulnerable; other students could laugh at me, or worse, make a stink about not being able to see the instructor because of my huge body. But I couldn't stomach the thought of being stuck in the back, either, and unable to see the instructor myself. As soon as class started, I felt myself coming alive. I'd never done Zumba before and it was an enchanting mix of Latin rhythms. It was different than a traditional dance class—there was no instruction, no counts, no breaking down of the movements. The instructor just went and you had to follow, but the thumping beats and sexy hip gyrations came naturally to me. When the hour-long class was finished, I was exhausted and my toes were numb. I started toward the door but then changed my mind and approached the instructor.

"I just wanted to tell you I had such a wonderful time. I used to dance and I've just lost eighty pounds and this was so fun."

"Used to dance? What were you just doing? No 'used to' about it!" she said.

"I would love to get a Zumba teaching license someday, when I get to my goal weight. I'm almost halfway there."

She asked for my name and said, "Whitney, I wouldn't say this if I didn't mean it. You should be teaching Zumba now." She handed me her card.

When I got to the car, I immediately called my parents and told them that an amazing Zumba instructor had just told me that I should be teaching it, after just one class! I looked up the website on the card and discovered they were offering a certification day in Raleigh the next week. Not allowing enough time to talk myself out of it, I whipped out my credit card and signed up.

A few days later I was sitting on the patio, drinking a detox tea with Ashley and screwing around on the Internet. I saw that a message had popped up on my OkCupid app. It was from a guy named Chad. Through conversation, I learned that he was an EMT and originally from California. He was cute, too—half white and half black, or "Halfrican," as he described himself on his profile, and husky. Well, let's be real, he was fat, but because we afford men different adjectives than women, he would most likely be described as husky. He asked me about my day, and I told him about my plans to get my Zumba license. "Cool," he wrote. "You'll have to teach me how to dance."

Chad asked me out to dinner the same day I would be going for my Zumba license. I would drive to Raleigh to complete my training and, if I was lucky, return home officially a Zumba instructor. I was shocked by how easily I learned and performed. There were women there who were older, some who were bigger. It definitely wasn't the Barbie Fitness Pageant I'd expected it to be. And eight hours later I headed back to Greensboro with my Zumba license in hand. Dinner with Chad was nice, and he kissed me at the end of night. I could see potential with him. One night, he asked me to go out with his friends, and the next morning, when he asked me to be his girlfriend, I accepted with no hesitation.

Coincidentally, my dissatisfaction with Target was soon alleviated. One night while I was at Heather and Jared's, Jared broached the idea of me joining the morning radio show he was part of, as they were looking for a new call screener who could not only execute the technical duties of the job but also be engaging on the air. Jared thought that I was funny and always had a crazy story to tell. A few days later, the host, Bob, called me in for an interview, and I started the next week. I scrambled, trying to learn my way around equipment and programs I'd never seen before, but I desperately wanted this job. Although it also paid me minimum wage, part-time (four-thirty to ten-thirty A.M.), it seemed way more fun and interesting than retrieving discarded candles and clothing from the pillow aisle at Target.

Bob explained to me that this would be a trial run and they'd call me "Intern Whitney," even though legitimate interns had to be fulfilling a school or college credit and could not accept payment. He explained that calling me an intern gave him an out if he decided I wasn't fit for the job. Since this job wasn't a sure thing, I continued working at Target, closing the store at ten at night, only to wake up at four the following morning. Bob joked that I was either the hardest-working person or the most broke person he'd ever met. In reality, I was both. Meanwhile, I continued to chase my weight-loss goal and increased my exercise in a bid to get over the plateau I was experiencing. I started training with Will every day, in addition to my solo exercise, and juggled my new relationship with Chad.

October 14, 2011: 91 pounds lost. I felt panicky. In my fantasy, I'd wanted to lose 100 pounds in six months. Considering I'd lost fifty in three months, I legitimately thought this was feasible. When the six-month mark passed, I adjusted my goal to 100 pounds in ten months.

"Anything other than that just isn't good enough!" I told Will. "I don't want to be one of those people who took an entire YEAR to lose 100 pounds!" As much as I hate to admit it now, I held prejudices against fat people. While I never would have dreamed of outwardly criticizing a fat person, I'd always tried to separate myself from them, thinking I wasn't one of them because I hadn't always been fat. I wasn't satisfied with being fat, I reasoned, because I'd been thin and I knew what life was like then. I knew what I was missing. Once I started to lose weight and saw how difficult it was for me to do so, I lost all sympathy for fat people who said they couldn't lose weight, especially the ones who didn't have a health condition that influenced it. I prided myself on being a different kind of fat person. The kind who had taken control of her life and who didn't make excuses. Anything was possible, if you wanted it bad enough—and I thought that fat people should want it bad enough. I absolutely believed that every fat person would commit themselves to losing weight if they truly understood how much better their life would be after doing so. And, as for me, having come so far, I couldn't understand what wasn't working anymore. Will examined our routines and thought that maybe I was doing too much exercise and not eating enough. I was defeated. I stopped recording my weight after that, but by mid-November, I'd quit my job at Target and lost my 100 pounds.

The same week, I received an email from Pratt notifying me of my scheduled audition. I'd completely forgotten about it, and meant to write them and cancel it. I was only halfway to my weight-loss goal and knew there was no way I was ready to audition for the dance therapy program. I talked it over with my dad, who reminded me that I didn't think I was ready to be a Zumba instructor, either, but look how that turned out. He admitted that I most likely shouldn't expect to be accepted, but that there was nothing wrong with attending the audition to get a sense of what I could prepare for the next time around. Because my trial at the radio station had no finite end, I was constantly on edge, worrying each day if I would be let go. With the future so uncertain, I took my dad's advice and booked both Chad and myself plane tickets to New York City for the last week in November.

While in New York, I enjoyed the bustling traffic, the diversity, and the heightened sense of being alive in the world, but I was a bundle of nerves as we took a taxi to Pratt. We located the building where the audition was to be held, and after slipping off my shoes and tightening my bun, I went to open the door to the dance studio.

"Don't watch," I told Chad, who could have peeked through a glass panel on the door. "I'm serious."

Even though I'd gotten my Zumba license, I'd never danced in front of Chad and couldn't imagine doing so. It felt way too vulnerable.

The audition went better than I expected. It was less intimidating and included more intuitive movement than I'd imagined. At the end, we gathered around to go over some common questions. Even though I felt decent about my audition, any fleeting thought of acceptance was erased by the admission statistics—that only a very small percentage of those who auditioned would make it into the program.

Afterward, we were each assigned a twenty-minute slot to visit the dean's office for an interview. Chad and I wandered around, kicking the fall leaves and looking at the funky sculptures on campus, while I waited for mine.

When it was my turn, I took my seat in the dean's small, cluttered office. She asked me an overarching question about my interest in the program and I answered, feeling like I was regurgitating the personal statements I'd sent with my application months earlier.

"Well," she cut in, when I paused to collect my thoughts, "I can already tell you that you're accepted into the program."

"What?" I squeaked, as the tears streamed down my face.

When I walked down the hallway toward where Chad was waiting, his expression was sympathetic.

"I'm sorry, baby," he said, enveloping me in his arms.

"I got in," I whispered through my tears.

"What? *What?* Yes!"

Having heard me sniffling through the walls, he naturally assumed the interview hadn't gone well. It didn't cross his mind (or mine) that I could be accepted on the spot.

The phone call to my dad afterward was one of my favorites.

"Ha!" he woofed. "Is there anything you can't do, girl?"

As we flew back home, I thought about my dad's question. I had to admit, there were things happening in my life that I would've dismissed as impossible, as a 229-pound woman. I'd acquired a fitness certification, graduate school admission, and a boyfriend. I knew there was something to be gleaned from all this (the inspirational quote "If not now, when?" comes to mind), but as much as I should have given myself credit for being a bad-ass, I was much more inclined to thank my lucky stars, attributing my success to outside circumstances rather than giving myself any credit. I decided against enrolling at Pratt and racking up a ton of student loans in favor of seeing where my radio job and my relationship with Chad would take me. The dean promised me that I could enroll any time I wanted, so I kept it in my back pocket. For the time being I would focus my energy on bulldozing through life until I reached my 199-pound weight loss goal, making me a nice, neat 130 pounds. But I never did achieve my 199-pound goal, nor did I ever take the dean up on her graduate school offer.

Within a few months my schedule became completely unmanageable. Due to my four-thirty start time at the radio station, working out in the morning was an impossibility. As soon as I got home around noon, I was so exhausted that I couldn't stand the thought of working out. I'd go back to sleep instead, and by the time I woke up, it was dinnertime and then the cycle repeated. Are these excuses? Yes. Sure, my life and schedule had changed dramatically, but we can always make time for what's important. And what was important to me *now* was my independence. Against my dad's better judgment, I took my savings from Korea and moved into a cheap two-bedroom apartment with Ashley.

I worked my ass off at the radio station. I loved my relationship with Chad. I loved having someone to share meals and conversations with. What I wanted was freedom from restriction—from calorie counting and unforgiving exercise routines. I felt like I was among the living again, cultivating a social life and enjoying my romantic one. I hung out with Chad's friends a lot and enjoyed their company. I even met a girl named Donna who I particularly liked. Needless to say, even though I didn't completely abandon working out or clean eating, I phased it out during the next year and the weight I'd lost started to come back. When my birthday rolled around that April, I'd gained thirty pounds, but I thought I could keep it under control.

My six-month lease would be up soon, and Chad and I had filled out all the paperwork to sign a lease of our own. On my twenty-eighth birthday I woke up to an *I love you!* message written on my mirror from Chad. He gave me a book I'd mentioned, a certificate for a massage, and a stuffed beaver (my favorite animal). That night two of Chad's girlfriends, whom I adored, threw me a little party. They brought me gifts and musical cat cards with sweet messages. As we played beer pong in the driveway, I announced to everyone that I was having a wonderful time. I felt special.

At some point a girl named Lisa pulled me to the side and said she'd heard I was moving in with Chad. I wasn't aware that he'd told his friends yet, but I confirmed the news. "Well," she began in a hushed voice, "I just want you to know that Chad said he wasn't sure about y'all." I thanked her for telling me but said I was sure it was some kind of misunderstanding. Her comment seemed so out of left field that I wasn't particularly worried about it. When Chad and I got in my car to leave, I brought it up, in a nonaccusatory tone. I hadn't been worried, but Chad's reaction made me so. He was overly defensive and denied ever saying anything like that, and he was angry at me for giving it any credence. The night ended poorly, in an argument, with both of us going our separate ways afterward, with me dramatically moaning about having to deal with this shit "on my birthday!"

Even though there had been a few red flags with Chad before, I still loved him. No one is perfect, I rationalized, and it wasn't like I didn't have my faults. I could be needy and overly sarcastic. Overall, Chad had been a loyal, supportive boyfriend, so when he swore to me that he'd never said he was unsure about us, I believed him. But I demanded that he confront Lisa because I couldn't understand why she would make up something like that for no reason. I sat upright between his legs in my bedroom while we watched a movie. The mood was still tense, and when Chad's phone vibrated, the text message to Lisa open, I looked down.

You should be thankful, she had written. *I could have told her what you really said . . . that you aren't attracted to her.*

Those words hit me like a ton of bricks. I jumped up and ran out of the sliding glass doors to the apartment balcony, and Chad followed.

"If that's how you feel," I said calmly, while trembling inside, "then I need you to leave." Chad backpedaled, assuring me that the only times he'd said that he wasn't attracted to me was right after I got back from the gym or when muscle soreness had me hobbling in pain. I was working myself to the bone, mostly to be attractive for Chad, and that had made me look unattractive to him. The irony wasn't lost on me. It was a complete slap in the face, just like the time I'd finished a grueling workout and walked outside the gym only to be called a fat-ass by a guy in a passing car.

"Then why do you want to have sex all the time?" I shouted back.

"It's not that big a deal! No one is attracted to someone a hundred percent of the time!"

"No. You do not talk about someone you love that way, behind their back, in public, as though it's a problem, when your behavior every day indicates the opposite. Fuck you."

The next day I called my dad. I felt lower than I had in years. Something unthinkable was coming into focus for me: losing a hundred pounds had not mattered. I was still at the mercy of other people's standards and expectations. I was flooded with hopelessness. When strangers and society-at-large called me fat, they didn't know that I'd just lost 100 pounds. When they accused me of being weak and lazy, they had no idea I spent hours at the gym daily, and when they advised me to eat better, they weren't aware that I was starving. And so I felt that, regardless, as long as my body was fat, I would be on the receiving end of judgment, both from strangers who didn't know better and intimate partners who did.

"It doesn't matter, Dad! None of it matters. Even if I lose another hundred pounds, it won't matter. Then I'll have loose skin and I'll always have cellulite and my boobs will be saggy. I already have wrinkles. Nothing, *nothing* can change that!"

More than feeling betrayed by and disappointed in Chad, I felt like I'd fooled myself. I'd thought that losing weight had been so productive and restorative. That each pound lost abated my insecurity a little bit more. I thought I'd been fixing myself, from the outside in. And yes, while I'd accomplished a lot besides pounds lost, none of it mattered if society and my own boyfriend couldn't accept me. Regardless of the work I thought I'd done, it all fell away in the eyes of others.

When I stopped by Chad's house, he started crying before he even asked if I was breaking up with him. I told him I didn't want to but that I felt shattered. Eventually he persuaded me to get in bed and he tried to make love to me, but my body heaved with sobs as he attempted to undress me. The next day at my house, I eyed the massage certificate, wondering if it might be just the thing to take my mind off things. But imagining another person looking at and touching my body made me shudder.

In the weeks that followed, Chad promised to make things up to me, but the incident was too big a blow. After a stressful month that climaxed with me screaming that I didn't love him, I broke up with him. Life got even more stressful when our radio host of twenty years was let go and Katie, Jared, and I were left to fend for ourselves at work. I took on new duties, a new title ("Producer Whitney"), and much more responsibility.

With all these changes, the tidal wave of self-doubt and depression crashed just like clockwork. Even after all the developments of the past year and a half, one thing remained true: my body was a problem. I was *still* fat, and the people who loved me, either consciously or subconsciously, couldn't deal with it.

8

BEING FETISHIZED
ISN'T FLATTERING

For the next six months the only saving grace I had was Donna, Chad's friend whom I'd met months earlier. We spent all our time together. She built me up when I was feeling low, she ate Chinese on Friday nights with me, she told me when Chad was sleeping with other people, and we laughed so hard together that we spit out our drinks. We gave each other pet names: she is Boo Boo and I am Boo Boo. I'm not sure whether we lack creativity or if we are so codependent that we have to go by the same name, but it works for us.

After a few months Donna encouraged me to get out into the dating world again, so back to OkCupid I went. This time I was quite a bit heavier and I didn't have as much luck on the site. Some examples of messages I received were (all spelling and grammar is theirs, not mine—I mean, come on):

What wonders the interwebs archive. You were cute till those full body pics. Cardio

Cute smile and XXL boobs yes please lol

your eyes smile are sexy hot I love thick wide curvy hip women hot. Have those? Online now?

So imagine my surprise when a message arrived in my in-box that fit all my criteria: the man who sent it was physically attractive (so much so that my knee-jerk reaction was to wonder if it was some kind of sick joke). Adequate spelling and grammar. (He exhibited comprehension of to/too/two, there/their/they're, and to top it all off, he used Oxford commas. Be still my heart.) College education. (He'd even been to more than one!) And perhaps the most important qualification in the arena of online dating: geography. Having once lived in my own hometown, he now lived in Asheville, a beautiful mountain town full of artists, breweries, and breathtaking nature. It was a few hours away, but definitely within driving distance, and it seemed like he visited Greensboro fairly often.

As I scrolled, my eyes darting across the screen from photos to paragraphs to compatibility questions, I learned that his name was Owen, he was into photography, and he studied international business in college. In one photo he wore linen pants and a crisp white dress shirt with the first few buttons undone and sleeves rolled up, standing in front of a Mediterranean-looking body of water. I almost had an orgasm before I could touch my fingers to the keyboard.

I threw my legs over the edge of the bed and turned my lights on. I looked at myself in the mirror. How could I respond to this dude? I sat back down on my bed, pulling my laptop over. I took a deep breath. I clicked on my own profile to remind me of what Owen had seen before he messaged me.

My self-summary:
I'm Whitney. I'm 28. I dance everywhere always and laugh way too loudly. I have an affinity for all animals, especially cats and beavers. Down to get turnt on every occasion. Good grammar turns me on more than your six-pack ever will.

What I'm doing with my life:

I'm a local producer and personality for a morning radio show. I dance; I read; I write; I hang out with my friends. I wonder what the hell else I'm supposed to be doing!

I'm really good at:

Dancing, meeting new people, untying knots, and spelling.

Clearly what I was not good at was keeping my cool when men who met my standards at first glance expressed the slightest bit of interest in me. Seriously, Whitney, I told myself. He wrote, *Hey Whitney! How are you? Message me if you want to get to know each other ;-).* He didn't propose marriage, for God's sake.

As I shakily crafted a response, I chided myself: You deserve a man who you find attractive. You deserve a man who piques your interest. You deserve a man who is smart and well-educated.

After exchanging a few OkCupid messages, I gave Owen my phone number and we texted for a couple of hours. He was intelligent, charming, and hadn't done the most dreaded thing—he hadn't asked me for "pics." When I realized it was one-thirty in the morning, I told him I had to go. My work week started in two and a half hours. As I lay in bed, my head spun with possibilities. Owen and I had covered a lot of ground in those few hours and he'd already tentatively suggested hanging out the next time he came to Greensboro. We continued texting throughout the following day, and when I woke up before the sun on Tuesday, I had a late-night text from him that read:

Whitney, I enjoy talking to you so much and your smile makes me smile every time I see it. I can't wait to meet you in person.

Reading those words made my heart jump. I knew I was getting way ahead of myself, considering we hadn't yet met, but I was so hungry for a partner. We solidified plans—he would come to town Friday night for our date. I ran through a mental checklist of everything I needed to do before then: clean room, clean apartment, buy a new outfit, completely clear my skin up, lose fifty pounds, increase the thickness of my hair by 75 percent (remember, PCOS thins your hair, that bitch), cultivate an interest in an obscure but relevant social issue, hang impressive art on the walls, shave entire body including face . . . It seemed doable, but I've always been an optimist.

I allocated Thursday after work as my date prep time, starting at noon and finishing whenever I was done. That way, all I would have to do on Friday was shower, obsess over meeting him, and pretend to relax. But, naturally, life got in my way. Everything that could go wrong went wrong. Thursday morning my coworker asked the intern and me to drive down to Raleigh, an hour and a half away, to interview the band Fun. and attend their concert that night. I had been a huge fan of the lead singer when he was in another band, called The Format, and I loved the Fun. singles currently playing on the radio. I didn't want to miss out on this opportunity, as any perks I enjoyed from being employed at the radio station were few and far between. I'd never interviewed or even met anyone famous before and I was clueless about where to start.

As I scrambled to think of questions to ask, I received intermittent texts from Owen, full of reassurances and encouragements. And then the dreaded question: he asked me for "pics." (A gateway to sexting, and a total romance-killer.) And not just any kind of pics—he wanted a full-body picture. I'd explained to him casually in our initial conversation that I'd lost a hundred pounds a year before but gained about fifty back, and that I felt I was on my way to self-acceptance but not there yet. In reality, had I actually weighed myself, I would have known I had gained more like seventy pounds. And I wasn't on that path to self-acceptance quite yet—rather, I was still driving to the forest where the path would eventually unfold. I stood in my apartment, looking at his text and realizing that I had literally never taken a full-body selfie. I didn't respond. He knew I was busy, so I could probably get away with not sending one. A few minutes passed.

I want to see your concert outfit, his next text prompted. Fuck. Now not only did I have to produce my first full-body selfie, I had to match the same level of style I'd seen in his photos. Owen was not only conventionally hot with his chiseled features and glittery eyes, but he was also stylish and well groomed. His hair was the ideal combination of careless and perfect. He wore expensive shoes and outfits just trendy enough to betray his fashion sense, but not so much that you'd think he was too materialistic. Then there was my outfit: a gray cowl neck sweater, black leggings from Walmart, and the only boots I owned, bought on clearance at least three seasons ago. Fuck it, I thought, racing through the apartment and judging my reflection in each mirror. None of them allowed me enough space to really get my entire body in lengthwise, but I finally settled on the one in the dining room, which allowed for midthigh up. I snapped a couple of photos, with my hip cocked and one hand on my comparably slim waist. As I flew down the stairs to my car, I sent them and then threw the phone in my purse to await his reaction.

As I was driving to the station to meet the intern, my thoughts went around in a ridiculous loop . . .

He's going to realize you're bigger than he thought. He's going to cancel. So what if he cancels? Then he's either a dick or he's not attracted to you. Better to know now. But if he just met me in person, I'd win him over with my personality. God, please, let this work. Let one thing work.

I didn't pull my phone out of my purse until I was in the station vehicle with the intern and on the highway to Raleigh. Then I knew I had to face it.

Damn. Those hips make me feel things. I'm glad I decided to come see you.

Before I could be relieved, I had to reexamine the photo and decide how much thinner and better it made me look than I did in real life.

We bantered playfully through text message on the way to Raleigh. When I got there, the intern and I conducted the interview, asking mostly lighthearted questions with some word association games thrown in, and had our pictures taken.

After the interview, the intern and I went for a beer at a restaurant next to the venue, as we had a couple hours to kill before the concert. I told Owen that we'd survived the interview and that we were going to have a drink. A couple hours later a text came through.

How's my pretty drunk girl?

Not drunk, I replied, feeling my face flush at his use of the word "my" and the possessiveness it implied. I then proceeded to get drunk at the concert. I was a sweaty mess and gathered my two hundred strands of hair into a bun within minutes. I danced and enjoyed the music and felt butterflies every time my phone lit up with a notification from Owen.

A girl I'd been chatting with was overly friendly and also conventionally attractive. For a brief moment I wondered if she was flirting with me, but I dismissed it. When the concert was over, she held my head close to hers and handed me her phone to enter my number. An hour later, in the passenger seat of the station car while the intern drove back to Greensboro, I received a text from her.

If you like girls, let me know. We could have some fun. :)

"Why?" I lamented to the intern, banging my head against the headrest. "Why do girls always like me?" I closed my eyes and hoped Owen would feel the same way when I met him the next day.

When I arrived home at two-thirty A.M., I plugged in my long-dead phone and was greeted with a barrage of texts from Owen, the kind you'd expect from a boyfriend. There was the *How's the concert?* text, followed by the *I hope you're having fun!* text, and then the concerned *Where are you? Did you get home safe?* text.

Yes, I replied, explaining that my phone had died. I told him about the concert and he asked me to send him my favorite Fun. song. I instead chose a Format song called "On Your Porch" and sent the YouTube link.

I like it, he texted back. *We should make out to it tomorrow.*

The next day, I walked into Katie and Jared's office for our daily postshow meeting. I was a nervous wreck for my upcoming date and extremely sleep-deprived. I collapsed into a chair.

"So tonight's the night, huh?" Katie asked me with a quick raise of her eyebrows.

"What's tonight?" Jared asked, not liking to be left out of any gossip, especially gossip that could provide fodder for the program.

"I specifically didn't tell you because I can't risk him finding out I'm talking about him on the radio."

"Who?" demanded Jared.

"This guy, he lives in Asheville."

"He's not even in our listening area! Who is he?"

Not one to keep exciting things to myself, I launched into the whole story, and Jared immediately demanded to see pictures of him.

"Oh no. There's no way," he said when I showed them. "There's gotta be something wrong with him. No offense, but he is way too good-looking."

Instead of being offended, I said, "I know." I was so tired and nervous that I was on the verge of tears, swimming in the anxiety of knowing Owen would be seeing me in person in mere hours.

"Whitney," Katie began in her usual diplomatic tone, "look, you're not going to know until you know. So get it together and quit worrying. Be yourself, have a good time, and if it's good, it's good. If not, on to the next."

She was right. I collected myself and left.

"Whitney!" Katie called from the office. I poked my head back in.

"And don't sleep with him!"

I nodded and drove home to attempt to get my shit together before seven. After taking one look at my apartment, I called in the reinforcements. Ashley was on the balcony having coffee.

"Oh, Lord," she said, assessing my harried appearance. "I have to work at five, so I won't be here to do your hair and makeup, but I'll help you clean."

"Perfect. Thank you. I love you," I said as she retreated inside for the cleaning supplies. I still wasn't sure I'd have enough time to accomplish everything I needed. I called my mother.

"Mom, seriously, you don't understand. This dude . . . I'm going to focus on my room and Ashley's going to do the kitchen, but maybe you could help me, like, dust the blinds or something."

"Whitney," she started in her Southern drawl, "if he's busy looking at the dust on your blinds, that's your first problem."

"Mom!" I shrieked, borderline hysterical. "Please. Please. *Please*. I want everything to be perfect. Don't you want grandchildren?"

"Why is he seeing your interiors on the first date?"

I let out an exasperated sigh. "He probably won't, Mom, but just in case we come here after dinner or something. I have literally five hours and fifteen minutes before I have to be in the shower. Please!"

Before hanging up, she made a sound that signaled she would give in to my request while reminding me she wasn't happy about it. For the next five hours we cleaned the apartment top to bottom.

Once Ashley had gone to work, I took my drenched, hungry, bleary body to the shower. I let the hot water run down my face as I tried to calm myself. After the shower I sat at my desk with a glass of wine and began applying makeup. I cursed my hair, which was neither wavy enough to be cute nor straight enough to not need to be straightened. Time was running out.

Owen texted, asking me about the restaurant I'd chosen. It was Korean and he'd looked up the menu online. *Want to meet me at 8?* I typed, furiously digging through the clothes in my closet. He agreed.

As I drove to the restaurant, still fifteen minutes away, I realized I hadn't scouted out the seating arrangements ahead of time. It had been a few months since I was there, and I was bigger now. Unsure of whether I would fit in the booths, I called Donna.

"Boo Boo!" I said breathlessly. "Can I fit in the booths there? Are they the kind attached to the wall or can I move them?"

"I think you can fit," she answered. "But I'm not sure. Maybe ask him to get a table."

"I'm sure he's already there!" Using voice-to-text, I messaged him, asking if he was already there, praying there were no typos.

I am, he replied. *Where are you?*

On my way! I said. *Sorry I'm late—bad first impression, I know.*

Then, realizing that if I couldn't change a potentially awkward situation, I wanted to at least be prepared. I asked, *Are you at a table or booth?*

A booth, of course :)

Great.

I parked at the restaurant with sweaty palms. When I walked inside, I saw him sitting at a booth, every bit as handsome as I expected. He stood to give me a hug. Miraculously, I slid into the booth with a couple inches to spare. We made small talk, which was easy enough. We talked about the side dishes that came with our food, and I made sure to pick at them, instead of devouring them like I wanted to. I hadn't eaten in twenty-four hours, but this was not the time to make it obvious. We playfully argued about the name of a Greek isle we'd both visited.

"I'm positive," I said, waving my metal chopsticks in the air. "It's Rhodes."

"You're cute," he said in response.

I laughed. "Thank you. You're cute. And handsome."

When we finished dinner, he asked if I wanted to get a drink. Not wanting to deal with any more unknown seating situations, I offered an alternative.

"We could just go to my house and watch a movie or something."

"That sounds good," he agreed as he leaned in toward me and kissed me.

I smiled. "Follow me?"

On the way back to my apartment I called Donna again with a feverish update. "He's normal. He's hot. Maybe the slightest bit of a lisp. He kissed me!" I barked.

"Whooo! Go Boo Boo, go Boo Boo!"

"Call you tomorrow!"

When I turned on the lights to let Owen into my apartment, he surveyed the illuminated living room. He walked to the couch, slowly turning around. "It's very tidy," he observed.

Dripping with satisfaction, I said flippantly, "Yeah, well, that's just the way I like it."

We sat down together on the couch for a few minutes before deciding to go to my bedroom. I was still incredibly nervous, and had been reserved all evening. My boisterous laugh and outgoing personality were hiding under a blanket of insecurity, most likely in the fetal position. I think I'd subconsciously decided that if I didn't show him too much of me, he wouldn't have anything not to like.

I changed into a comfy gray Old Navy T-shirt and invited him under my down comforter. He balanced my computer on his lap and rattled off some Netflix selections.

"Oh, whatever, I'm easy," I said, although nothing could be further from the truth. When it comes to entertainment, I am painfully picky. The choice of movie proved irrelevant, because before long he put the laptop on my desk and pulled me close to his chest, kissing me on the head. When I looked up, a full-on make-out session ensued. Between kisses, he positioned himself on top of me and sat back on his knees between my legs.

"Hmm-mm," I said, pulling him back up to my face. I was determined to keep the night relatively PG, not because of a commitment to appearing chaste, but so my body wouldn't scare him off on the first date.

I awoke early the next morning with Owen softly snoring in my darkened room. I went to McDonald's and scarfed down a sausage, egg, and cheese biscuit and answered Katie's texts about how the night had gone. *God, it feels good to eat,* I thought.

When I got back to the apartment, coffee in hand, Ashley was rummaging through the kitchen. Owen came out briefly before going into the bathroom.

Oh yeah, Ashley mouthed, drawing it out so big that I could see her molars.

I know! I mouthed back.

I was hosting a Zumbathon in High Point that morning, so I brushed my teeth and dressed quickly, telling Owen he was welcome to take his time and let himself out. After the Zumbathon was over, Donna and I went to Panera to evaluate the previous night.

"You seem calm, Boo Boo," she noted, biting into a panini.

"Yeah, it was . . . nice. Comfortable. Maybe too comfortable. I felt pretty subdued. He'll probably never text me again."

No sooner was that out of my mouth than my phone dinged. *Last night was fun.*

"Wait five minutes," Donna instructed in a stern voice.

After four, I responded: *Yeah, it was.*

Said Donna: "Add a smiley face."

After continuously texting throughout the next week, Owen sent me some screen shots of fat women, fatter than me, in skimpy lingerie. One of the pictures was a fat woman posing with a cupcake. The photos made me uncomfortable for more reasons than one.

First off, I was uncomfortable looking at someone like myself naked. That's why I didn't, even in the privacy of my own home. I couldn't stand the thought that I looked anything like these women in the pictures, even though I was pretty sure I did. I stood on my knees like one of the girls, naked on my bed, and checked out my reflection in the mirror over my dresser. To my horror, I looked almost identical to the soft-core porn image on my phone. The fat, the cellulite, the flabbiness, it all made me sick to my stomach.

Second, as I told Owen, *I don't like the food stuff.* I'd spent so many years trying to hide the fact that I needed nutrition and sustenance like a normal person. I certainly didn't like the idea of publicly indulging in cupcakes for the sake of some gross erotic fantasy.

Oh, I didn't notice the food stuff, Owen wrote back. Likely story. Then I had a thought that knocked the wind out of me.

Wait . . . I typed quickly. I knew that Owen was a photographer. *Do you work for this website? Are you trying to get me into porn? Is that what this is?*

It would make sense. I had thought it was weird that Owen was interested in me. Maybe he'd just been buttering me up the whole time, trying to manipulate me, so that by the time he turned on a light and shoved a cupcake in my face, all he'd have to do is say, "Action!"

What?! No. His texts started coming in quick succession. *I've never even shot a naked woman in the studio. Ever.*

I told him I thought one of the girls was pretty, but I didn't have smooth skin like hers. Owen wouldn't know that because he'd only been with me in the dark. Now that I realized there were pretty fat girls doing porn, I felt doubly inadequate. Not only was I not a hot girl, but suddenly I didn't feel like a hot fat girl, either.

Baby, I think you're beautiful. I would never have sent you these if I thought it would upset you. I supposed I believed him, but I was still so confused about these photos and what Owen saw in them. It couldn't be the same as what he saw in me . . . could it? There was only one thing to do: I needed to consult my sisterhood.

"Boo Boo . . . no. There's something wrong."

"I know," I said. "I know it's weird as fuck, but like, I think he just likes big women."

"But has he said that, though?" Donna asked, looking at me quizzically the next day in my bedroom.

"Well, no, he's said he likes all kinds of women. But why else would he like the bbw sites? Normal men don't like women like us."

"Well, exactly," she reasoned. "That's why something has to be wrong with him."

Replaying this conversation with my best friend makes me want to howl from equal parts laughter and sadness. Knowing everything I know now, it makes me sad to think we both simply could not wrap our heads around a conventionally attractive, intelligent, "normal" guy liking big women, exclusively or not. And the humor of it all isn't lost on me, either. It's so obvious: not only did Owen pursue me, a big woman, sexually, but he went so far as to send me pictures of other big women that aroused him, sexually. It would seem quite clear that he liked big women, sexually, but here were two college-educated women breaking a sweat trying to decipher what it all meant.

Sometimes the best explanation is the simplest one. Here was a normal guy, attracted to fat women. Shocking, I know.

A few days later Ashley and I ordered a pizza, and when I answered the door, I recognized the guy delivering it but I didn't let on. I always found it mortifying to run into people from my past because the person who gets fat after high school is a running joke in every social circle. But the guy recognized me, too.

"Didn't we go to high school together?" he asked.

"Um, maybe," I bluffed. "What's your name?"

"Buddy."

"Oh! Buddy! Of course! How are you?" I hadn't seen Buddy since I was eighteen, but he was a friend of my high school boyfriend, Shawn, and worked on some of the same shows as I did at the Carolina Theatre. Later that night, while chatting with Owen, I told him about it. Turns out he knew Buddy and told me a story of a time recently when they'd competed for the same girl, when Owen lived in Greensboro.

"I bet he wants to sleep with you," Owen teased.

"Ew, he does not." I shot him down, but I saw a twinge of jealousy emerge in Owen. So when Buddy and I became Facebook friends, when he invited me to his birthday dinner, and when he asked me to give his mom a birthday shout-out on the radio, I made sure to mention these events to Owen to gauge his reaction, as a litmus test of his feelings for me. The verdict: Owen was at least a little jelly.

I was eager for Owen to visit again, but I had the sinking feeling that he and I weren't going to amount to much. In the weeks that followed, conversation became sparse, sometimes absent for days at a time, and often turned sexual when we did talk. I'd been so shy and reserved on our first date, so timid and afraid of messing anything up, that I often felt like he didn't actually know me at all. But he was coming back to Greensboro at the end of December, and we made plans to go out again.

When he got into town, earlier than expected, he asked if he could just come over. I told him no, that I still had to shower and I wasn't comfortable. The truth? I didn't want any excuse for him to try any funny business and be stuck naked with him in the daylight. I was trying to impress him, not run him off, after all. He wanted to go to the movies, and my more pressing concern was that he drove a smaller car and I wasn't sure I would be able to fit comfortably in it. He persisted, but I finally convinced him to go in my 4Runner. As we walked into the movie theatre, I marveled at how this beautiful man was walking next to me in public on a Friday night, when people were sure to assume we were on a date! We saw *Django Unchained,* which was not only a great movie, but also quite long, which allowed me lots of time to revel in the moment.

When we got back to my place, I realized I was okay with him touching me, as long as he couldn't see the curves he was running his hands over. At one point he smacked my butt, and instead of feeling humiliated, I let myself enjoy it.

The next day was New Year's Eve, and in the morning we woke up, naked, and lounged in bed for hours. We had sex. We talked about photography. He dissected my fancy camera, showing me what each feature was used for. We had more sex. But eventually, when he announced that it was time for him to hit the road, I knew I wouldn't be seeing him for a long time, if not for good. As much as I wished I could date Owen, I could sense that he didn't feel anything for me, and I couldn't blame him. In an effort to be likable, I'd muted my entire personality. And because I wasn't being me, I couldn't see *him,* either. Everything about Owen was great on paper, and the sex was 8/10, but I knew that was that.

I wished I could believe that the kind of man I wanted could be attracted to me. I knew I wouldn't accept myself until I was either thin or could somehow come to terms with being fat. And I wasn't ready. As he gathered his things and talked about going to a New Year's Eve party, I made a resolution: the next time I met an Owen, I wanted to be ready.

I began to throw myself into work. Our show was now called *Jared and Katie in the Morning,* and it was a success. Without our old host, Bob, we had made a concerted effort to use our new-found creative freedom in fun and innovative ways. We were now in control of our content, and we loved it. I started a You-Tube channel for the show and got more active on social media.

In February, the "Harlem Shake" was sweeping the digital landscape, and we were scheduled to have Dustin Diamond, better known as Screech from *Saved by the Bell,* in the studio for an interview. Afterward, we convinced him to participate in our own "Harlem Shake" video and he obliged, even inviting us to his comedy show that evening in High Point.

Jared and I attended, and Donna came along. When it was over, as we sat chatting, Dustin announced that he wanted breakfast, so we hit up a twenty-four-hour diner. Say what you want about him and his tabloid headlines, but I found him to be one of the nicest, most genuine guys I'd met in a long time, fa-mous or not. You know how they say you can judge a person by how he treats the waitstaff at a restaurant? This same logic ap-plies, but substitute a fat/not conventionally pretty/differently abled woman. One of the things that struck me hardest after gaining so much weight so quickly is that most men never seemed to want to talk or pay attention to me anymore. And I don't mean overt sexual attention. I'm not offended when I don't get catcalled or when guys don't hang all over me at a drunken party. In other words: I don't care if you don't want to sleep with me. But I do care about all the other benign interac-tions that suddenly go missing. And I couldn't remember the last time a guy seemed interested in talking to or getting to know me without an ulterior motive.

This realization made me sad and caused me to reevaluate

every relationship I'd had with men in the past, especially the ones I hadn't thought of as romantic or sexual. Were they only being nice in order to get something in return? Had every pleasantry been a bid to get out of the dreaded friend zone and into my pants? (Side note: the "friend zone" is not a real place, but more on that later. Prepare your maps.) Now that men typically didn't want to have sex with me, they seemed to want nothing to do with me, period. It was as if I didn't even exist.

But that wasn't what I experienced with Dustin. He was kind, polite, and genuinely interested in conversation. And honestly, he seemed a little lonely. Obviously, his heyday as Screech had long since passed, but he was still famous, right? My ordinary-person mentality had difficulty understanding that being famous didn't equate to happiness any more than losing weight had for me. (This is also something I would later gain a personal understanding of, when I became "famous" myself.) Come to think of it, the only other "nice guy" I'd met who didn't devote all his time to getting into my pants was Buddy, which is precisely why I wanted him in my life.

Our "Harlem Shake" video didn't go viral, but we were having fun expanding our horizons. I was in charge of filming, editing, and posting videos for the station's YouTube channel. I taught myself how to use iMovie and bought the cheapest decent video camera I could find at Best Buy. It was exhilarating to learn a new skill and to use my creativity, and more than that, it was fun being silly every day. We were always on the hunt for new ideas. Jared had seen some of the dance videos I'd posted on my own Facebook page before I joined the radio, and he suggested I do some more, but he told me to choose Top 40 hits like we played on our station. And we needed a catchy title. "What about 'A Fat Girl Dancing'?" he proposed. My initial reaction was lukewarm.

"Look, it has everything," he continued. "Think about what's popular on YouTube: pop music, dance videos, fat people—but then when they see you can actually dance, it'd be a cool surprise."

I could admit that it seemed like a good idea, but my gut reaction was to flinch at the word "fat." Talking about my weight had become a staple of our morning program, and I played my size mostly for laughs, lamenting my dating life and experiences as a fat woman. I had never before been comfortable calling myself fat—not because I was in denial about it, but because I didn't want to acknowledge it at all. Discussing it on our morning show took the edge off. It allowed me to be open about it and hear feedback from our listeners. For example, one morning I told a story of taking my shirt off in hot yoga, and how I received a couple wayward glances from much fitter women who were also in just their sports bras.

Jared posed the question, "Are you okay with a fat person taking their top off in a group exercise class?" The calls flooded in, and the majority of callers, male and female, echoed the same sentiment.

"If she's exercising, who am I to judge?"

"Absolutely, she shouldn't be ashamed!"

"Yes, working out is for fitness, not for appearance!"

Jared enjoyed playing devil's advocate when it came to matters of my weight, often expressing the negative opinion I experienced in my daily life. As a heavy guy struggling with weight himself, he readily acknowledged the double standard when it came to men and women, but also made no effort to change his line of thinking. "Lucky for me!" he would say.

I'd been self-identifying as fat for a while and getting positive comments from listeners as well as social media messages thanking me for discussing my weight in a frank manner. So I decided that *A Fat Girl Dancing* would be fine. Actually, I thought, it was brilliant.

But far from purposefully promoting body-positivity (at this point, I'd never even heard of that term), I just thought it would make for a fun feature on our YouTube channel and got to work posting the first official Fat Girl Dancing video in February to Macklemore & Ryan Lewis's "Thrift Shop." I was a huge Macklemore fan, and Donna and I had used free tickets from the radio station to go see him in concert on a weeknight. To my horror, I could not fit in the coliseum chairs, so I encouraged Donna to stay put, while I walked to the top of the arena and asked the ushers if there was any chair, even a plain folding one, that I could set up. They told me that I couldn't block the aisle and there was no other kind of chair in the building. This seemed incredibly odd to me, as we were in the coliseum of our capital city. And the man had told me there were no chairs without ever going to look or asking someone on a walkie-talkie to check. My common sense tells me that there HAD to be a chair in that building, but that he just wasn't concerned with getting it for me. I wonder if he would have accommodated me differently if I'd had a broken leg or some other malady that was "not my fault." So I had to stand there at the top of the arena for the entire concert, my feet aching with pain by the time it ended.

The "Thrift Shop" dance video garnered an array of both positive and negative comments from our listeners.

> I hope she's on the bottom floor!

> I give that performance an 8 . . . on the Richter scale!

Reading those comments made my face burn, but I didn't feel like a joke. Of course, I had absolutely no idea that these videos would eventually spark my career.

This burgeoning creativity, increased responsibility, and a recent pay raise ($8.50 an hour!) were all that was keeping me going. My personal life was in shambles. Even with the raise, I had depleted my savings from Korea, and making under $15K a year was just not enough for me to pay rent, bills, gas, groceries, and still be able to afford a coffee and a weekly dinner or night out with my friends. I'd had no luck with online dating, and the bigger I got, the more insane the guys' messages became.

Sure, there were the staples—the offensive "pretty face" messages; the annoying "hi" and nothing more messages; and the "your fat" ones, which insulted my penchant for correct grammar more than anything else. I'd gotten nasty messages before, but they were becoming more intense in content and frequency. For example, after leaving a message unanswered for a few days, I woke up to a second try (this is verbatim!):

> Guess u full of shit then. You should really make it known on your profile so people don't waste their time. LMAO. SMH. You should really look at yourself and realize your DEFINITELY not a prize, just sum lard ass cum bucket and will always be. The one on someone shoulder but never a main squeeze. Have fun on here. I hope some redneck slits your throat.

Messages like this shocked me and weighted down my already sinking spirit. Not because I was personally offended by clearly crazy people on the Internet, but because these were the same people living in the real world. They were *someone's* father, brother, ex-boyfriend. I reported and blocked such accounts, but they hurt my heart. I ached for myself and for other women in the world who experience what I've experienced. Facing financial and emotional distress, the last thing I needed was online abuse. I'd begun isolating myself socially. A year and a half since I'd stopped training with Will, I had gained back *all* the weight (I was 330 pounds at this point), and I felt out of place in bars and restaurants.

When we instituted a "Drunk Trivia" segment on the program, I enthusiastically volunteered to give up a Friday night and corralled Donna and the intern and headed to the bar where

Buddy bartended, although he wasn't working that night. As I used my phone to record drunk strangers answering questions—"Who's the vice president?" or "What's the order of the colors of the rainbow?"—I noticed out of the corner of my eye that a guy was chatting up Donna. Because Donna is a strikingly beautiful, friendly Asian woman, it is unheard of for her to not get hit on. I can't count how many times a sloppy drunk has lurched over to her to tell her she looks like a geisha and to say *"Koni-chiwa."* This behavior really pisses Donna off. It pisses me off, too.

This particular guy she was talking to seemed nice enough, though, and I caught snippets of their conversation. Donna was telling him she wanted to go to graduate school for psychology. He seemed interested. When I was done with my group, I thought he'd be a good choice to interview next, as he was already immersed in conversation with my friend (i.e., he'd probably be willing). But when I got a better look at him, I felt a shot of adrenaline course through my body. I knew his face from an OkCupid interaction a year and a half earlier. Basically, the dude messaged me and I didn't answer, so he was shitty to me about my weight. Then a year later he was shitty to me again about my weight because he forgot that he'd done it to me before.

I figured I had two options: I could pull Donna away from him and then avoid him for the rest of the night. Or, I could approach him and give him a piece of my mind. My heart raced at option two, but I was at my wit's end with assholes, so without further debate, I walked straight over.

"Hey! Do you want to do some drunk trivia?" I asked him.

"Sure!" he replied, with Donna still by his side.

"Great. What's your name?"

"Luke." I fucking knew it.

"Well, Luke, I'm Whitney and actually I know who you are."

His face was blank, but his body language indicated he was nervous.

"You don't remember me? From a couple months ago, on OkCupid—you told me I was too fat?" He remembered. Donna's mouth nearly hit the concrete floor as she put together what was happening.

"Yeah, so I'm an asshole . . ." He trailed off.

"Yes," I agreed. "You are an asshole, and I thought you should look at me face-to-face instead of spewing your bullshit on the Internet."

Because I wasn't playing nice and accepting his apology (not that you could really even call it that), Luke got visibly agitated.

"I can't help that you're fucking 300 pounds."

In my head I was thinking, Okay, actually thirty pounds over that, but awesome.

His voice was rising and the dozens of people out on the patio began to take notice.

I can't remember what I said back, but then Luke got closer to me and I could feel my adrenaline pumping.

"You're just a fat fucking bitch!" he shouted, inches away from my face. Audible commotion from the patiogoers followed, but no one stepped up or stepped in. Luckily, with that off his chest, Luke turned and went inside. Minutes later I was still shaking.

"Come on, Boo Boo, let's go," Donna said, grabbing my arm.

A year earlier I probably would have been out the door on my way to the car by then, crying about being mistreated. Then again, a year ago, my embarrassment over being fat in the first place would have prevented me from calling attention to it in public, especially if that meant confronting a man. I was totally fed up with being mistreated for being fat. I was coming to terms with being a fat woman, and it wasn't the worst thing in the world. In that moment I knew for sure that I wasn't the person I was a year ago.

"No, fuck that," I declared. "He can leave."

I was committed to standing my ground, but I was also fearful of how Luke might react the next time we were face-to-face. Neither Donna nor I knew how to physically protect ourselves should the need arise, so I called Buddy, even though he wasn't working, to let him know what had happened. Buddy and I were just beginning to be friendly again, but I knew that since he worked there, he wouldn't stand for incidents like this, and certainly not incidents that involved me.

When Buddy arrived twenty minutes later, Luke had slipped out the back. A girl approached me and told me that she admired how I'd stood up to him, that she listened to me on the radio, and that I inspired her. It occurred to me that by empowering myself, I could empower other women, even those who still remained silent in moments that called for outrage. I left feeling proud, strong, and accomplished.

The next day I woke up to an OkCupid message from some lame username with 69 on the end.

Nice tits. Wanna fuck?

After I wrote back, telling him he was wildly inappropriate, he sent back:

Sorry. Your a fat bitch and it was your only good feature.

Would it ever end?

Several weeks later, Luke, who, it turns out, was a regular, had the audacity to show up at Buddy's bar again. Buddy approached him with his drink order and said, "You were highly disrespectful to my friend Whitney Thore."

"Man," Luke interjected. "She totally just—"

Buddy slammed the beer down on the table. "If you ever look at her again, we're gonna have a problem."

That April, Buddy came to my aid again, to help me move out

of my apartment and back into my parents' house. I'd concluded that no matter how backward and immature it felt, the smartest financial decision was to move back in with Mom and Dad. It was the only financial decision, really. I was nursing a major crush on Buddy and was elated that he'd come through for me. My parents repainted and recarpeted the playroom for me. I appreciated this gesture, as it spared me from moving back into my old bedroom, still fully furnished in my then-teenage style. The playroom was just inside the garage and would hopefully allow me to feel a little more independent.

"Just ignore us if you want to!" they joked.

Without rent to pay, I felt somewhat relieved, but was still struggling with the feeling that I was not only stuck, but perhaps in a downward spiral. The day after I moved back in with my parents was the eve of my twenty-ninth birthday, and I got really drunk and came home to sob myself to sleep. The next morning my mom gave me a gift that would prove to be prophetic: a necklace with a square pendant that read: "Something good is going to happen." It was a nice gesture, but I was hyperfocused on one question: when?

I enjoyed my job, but it wasn't without its problems. Working in morning radio meant an unforgiving daily schedule, a consistent lack of sleep, and lots of uncomfortable situations. While I felt that Jared, Katie, and I worked almost flawlessly as a team, it could be awkward, to say the least, to share so much of your personal life with hundreds of thousands of people. While the majority of the on-air ribbing was fine, there were times for all of us when a segment could morph from funny to unexpectedly hurtful. Any conventional lines of separation between my personal life and work were blurred, if not invisible. Sometimes my friends, family, and even listeners would ask me why I put up with all the fun that was made at the expense of my weight. I reckoned that I had thick enough skin to deal with it, that it was for entertainment purposes, and that the same conversations that reeked of sexism and fat-hate would continue with or without me, so I might as well be thankful to have a voice in the conversation. But many days it all added up to hopeless tears streaming down my face as I began my drive home.

But soon my experience with morning radio got even *weirder*. In addition to the Fat Girl Dancing videos, we also filmed a segment every week called Torture Tuesday, where we chose some cruel and unusual punishment to enact on our intern. Such videos included waxing his chest hair and arranging a meeting between him and a dominatrix. On one particular Tuesday we decided I'd give him a "massage." This massage entailed me walking on his back and doing whatever I pleased. Surprisingly, the YouTube video that chronicled the event was gaining some traction online, more so than others, and we didn't know why. Then came an email from a man in Michigan:

> Whitney, I watched your massage video and I would love a massage like that. I would be happy to have you perform a similar massage on me if you want to buy a plane ticket. I am free for this any time.

And the messages kept coming. Soon I was getting friend requests from all over the U.S. and the world. We interviewed an Italian guy named Manuel who said I had the most beautiful body he'd ever seen and would love if I'd join him next month in Colorado when he would be there for a vacation. Then there was the guy who called in to tell us about a "bash" that was being held exclusively for fat women and their admirers and extended an invitation to me.

"Their admirers." Let that sink in. We had admirers? I had a flashback to the photos Owen had sent me. I was so confused and turned off by this, but enjoyed the radio fodder it provided. Then came the message from Matt. To be completely transparent, the first thing that caught my attention about Matt's message was his appearance. At over six feet, with a perfectly muscled body, smooth dark skin, and bright white teeth, he was not the typical man who messaged me online looking for a date. He made no mention of sex or other inappropriate suggestions in his message. He appeared smart and we had easy conversation. After sending several messages back and forth, my curiosity got the best of me.

Not that it matters really, but how did you find me? Our YouTube channel was not well known by any means (right now, the subscriber list barely tops 17K), and the digital material we created was mostly intended for our listening audience.

I really don't want to creep you out, Matt answered. But I demanded to know the information and promised I wouldn't be weird about it. The next message included a link to a forum where men posted photos of women they lusted after. *I knew you'd find us someday,* he added.

The next click led me down a rabbit hole. It took me to a thread devoted entirely to me. All my dance videos were there. There were before and after photos of me, chronicling my weight gain, and the comment sections were littered with users who pointed out my physical perfection (yes, sister, perfection) and moaned about their wishes for me to keep gaining, as well as what they would do during a night alone with me. Their fantasies ranged from having good old-fashioned sex with me, to me "squashing" them, to them feeding me. I didn't have the guts to specifically research every act that was listed, but deductive reasoning and context clues gave me a clear insight into the initially frightening world of fat fetishism.

I'm not a prude by any means, and my sexual history would surely elicit a flushed face and a horrified "Whee-it-ney!" from Babs (my mother), but my experimental tendencies have faded and I've realized that I'm largely okay with a vanilla sex life. Blindfolds, fuzzy handcuffs, and sex toys within a monogamous sexual or romantic relationship? Bring it on. But bring it once every few months, please. I'm basic and that's fine, but being suddenly thrust into the fetish world without having done anything to purposefully put myself there was dizzying.

There were so many emotions to deal with. There was utter surprise, as I was still digesting the concept that there were men in the world who preferred fat women specifically. Then there was an element of flattery, as I had felt almost completely deprived of positive sexual attention for all of my adult life. But the emotion that demanded my attention the most was mild disgust. My knee-jerk reaction is that it's gross and sleazy to saddle an unwilling or unknowing participant on the Internet with overt sexual attention. After all, I hadn't intended any photos or videos of me to be used in anyone's spank bank, so a forum designed to share this type of material made me feel violated. I felt objectified. It was the same feeling I had when I was walking down a sidewalk at age thirteen, on my way into a store to meet my dad, and there was a grown man pedaling his bike in the parking lot.

"Those are a delicious pair of britches!" he'd called out. Followed by, "The next time I see you, I'm going to hug you like I know you!" I was too young to identify this interaction as sexual harassment, but I knew by the way my dad bolted out of the store in search of the guy that it was wrong.

The attention from the forum also reminded me of my junior and senior years of high school, when I was small enough to be conventionally pretty and drove a Jaguar. Stoplights were a place of supreme discomfort, filled with catcalls and suggestive flicks of the tongue above car windows rolled halfway down. All the weight I had gained afforded me a certain amount of protection from a lot of this kind of harassment, but I began to be harassed in a different way. It seemed men either wanted me to satisfy their sexual urges or wanted to tell me they were mad at me for not being attractive enough to them to satisfy their sexual urges.

What a lose/lose! I'd never imagined that my current figure would have men salivating, but hey.

One Saturday night I attended a friend's wedding and brought Donna along as my date. There, at the wedding, an incredibly significant event unfolded that no one else would notice but me. This interaction marked the beginning of my rapid ascent into the fluffy, shiny nirvana of body-positivity.

As Donna and I were posing for a photo, I instructed the photographer—as I always did: "More face, less fat!" But then, without even realizing it, I corrected myself.

"Actually, do full body, please!"

As I examined the photos on the way home, I felt a jolt. I still critiqued the photo in my mind, thinking I should have worn a shawl to cover my arms and employed some body language tricks to visually slim myself, but I didn't say these thoughts out

*Dancing at my friend's wedding with bald spots showing
and sweat dripping (2013).*

loud. Because saying them out loud would validate them and I was having a bit of an a-ha moment. Far from becoming a fire, the spark was fragile and wavering. But it was definitely lit.

When we got back to my parents' home, my mother had uncharacteristically cooked some food and left it in the fridge. Babs is a better cook than she will ever take credit for, but Hunter and I departing for college signaled a shift (perhaps a relief, really) in her that meant meals became basically soups and sandwiches unless it was Christmas Eve. Boo Boo and I were starving; neither of us had eaten at the wedding, so we were giddy over the mashed potatoes, meat loaf, and broccoli casserole we'd happened upon at midnight. When Matt texted me and asked what I was eating, I sent him a picture.

Mmm. I bet you love to eat that Southern cooking, he replied. I responded honestly and without thinking.

Actually, I rarely eat food like this. I'm sure I eat waaaaay healthier than my figure would cause you to believe.

This statement was true, but it was also intended to preserve my image the way I had always wanted to be seen, which was not as a caricature of a fat person who stuffs her face and sits on her ass all day. Once I hit send, it dawned on me. Matt wasn't "mmming" over my meat loaf the same way people do on Instagram. He most likely didn't have a proclivity for the Food Network. *He was turned on!* He wanted me to agree with him and tell him about how I loved indulging myself in copious amounts of buttery, fatty food. Whoa.

I had to sit down to evaluate. Against all my better judgment and my instinct to shut all of this down, I was . . . turned on? No, I couldn't be. This was weird. Why did it kind of feel good?

It's easy for me to see why now. After a decade of being hated, humiliated, and ostracized because of my body, having it appreciated and viewed as sexy was disarming and somehow felt safe. Afraid to look like a pig, I'd be committed with any other guy to denying that I ate at all. I had been, for ten years, the stereotypical girl eating only a salad on the first date.

Matt later called in to the radio to explain his attraction to me. He described my bouncing belly, my jiggling thighs, the overall vastness of my body and how there were unlimited areas to explore. When Matt said I was soft, it took on a different meaning. There was no connotation of weakness. He eroticized every part of my body; each fold of fat multiplied pleasure, and he was as excited by love handles as he was by breasts. Matt had an uncanny way of turning everything I'd been taught to believe and perceive on its head, resulting in a total paradigm shift. A flaw became fabulous, depending on the beholder. Even stretch marks signified improvement rather than decline.

And the thing about feeling beautiful is that it is important. Beauty is subjective and will always be, but when we feel attractive as people, it impacts the way we go about our lives. It impacts the way we view the world and the way the world views us. My point: while physical preferences are definitely a thing, how attractive we feel greatly determines how attractive others perceive us to be.

Matt equated publicly expressing interest in fat women with coming out of the closet. Obviously, oppressions aren't comparable and, while he would have been looked down upon for liking fat women, Matt would have always been legally able to marry one. But still, when he told me about the serious flak he received from family and friends, my heart ached for him. I thought about the lengths men from my past had gone to in order to distance themselves from me, to hide or diminish our relationship. None of them had dated anyone my size before, and their browser history would corroborate that it was thin women, not fat women, who turned them on. And yet, all of them made some kind of exception for me.

Men had previously told me: "I've never liked a big girl,

but . . ." But *what*? Was it my personality that drew them in? Was it my pretty face that made me attractive enough? I didn't want to be someone's exception or experiment anymore.

Matt was attracted to me, and because my fatness was openly discussed and not avoided, I felt more at ease. The more I saw how much fortitude it took for him, especially as a living Ken doll, to publicly honor his natural desires for fat women, the more I started to respect and draw strength from him. Having the strength to rip Cindy Crawford and Pamela Anderson off the bedroom walls of his brain in favor of what turned him on was admirable. But to be clear, I'm not out to martyr Matt for seeking fat women to satisfy his natural sexual urges, and anything negative he experiences as a result of liking fat women doesn't compare to what I experience *being* a fat woman, but I am always down for people being unashamed of who they are and what they like.

Matt was the first inside look I had at men who loved fat women, but there were plenty more to come. I was no longer even half surprised by the strange and unorthodox requests that came my way. I even signed up for a website specifically designed for feeders, feedees, and fat admirers, though I specified in my profile that I was fat but not interested in being fed or fattened up. I'd hoped some decent guys would be on that site, more so because they'd find fat women there, and less because they had a fetish. But I was sorely disappointed. I would start talking to a guy who seemed cool only to have him skip straight from his favorite color straight to his desire to strap me to a bed and force-feed me ice cream.

Although my experience with Matt had made me consider men with a fat fetish as viable dating options, I was quickly forced to reconsider. Let me be clear: there's a lot going on here and I don't pretend to have it all figured out. When does a sexual preference become a fetish? Why do we demonize men who strictly like fat women but think nothing of men who strictly like skinny women? Do we label one group of men as having a fetish and the other not, based on what the cultural norm is? Did the men who painted Rubenesque women of the 1900s have a fetish? Why do we allow men less threatening fetishes, like foot fetishes, but lose our shit when a man wants to sample sex with women of a plumper variety?

Further still, does the ridicule men who like fat women endure force them into an isolation that breeds closeted desires and fetishistic tendencies? All the men I came to know from the forums and sites (and there were many) told me stories like Matt's: for as long as they could remember, they'd been attracted to fat women. Inevitably, there was some pivotal playground or lunchroom moment when their peers found out and mockery and public embarrassment followed. And so began the pattern of keeping it secret, of dating thin women so no one would suspect what they were actually into, some going so far as to carry this facade into marriage, all the while scouring the Internet for big women who would fulfill their desires while their wives slept. I heard stories of breakups caused by conventionally attractive thin women stumbling upon images in their boyfriends' computers that forced them to question whether the entire basis of their relationship—their presumed mutual attraction—had been a lie. Apparently, to realize that your boyfriend wanted to fuck fat women is to realize that he is sick and perverse and you'd better get out as soon as possible.

I knew some things: it was possible for me to love my body and genuinely find it attractive. Even though I had spent my whole life fighting against the notion that fat could be attractive, I had somehow arrived at that very conclusion. It was almost as if all I'd had to do was *really* consider it, and then—once I knew it was possible—I could believe it was true about myself. But that didn't mean entering into a relationship with a self-identified fat fetishizer was the solution for me, either. I couldn't get down with a man's desire to control me or manipulate my body for his pleasure.

While I *was* becoming progressively less concerned with the number on the scale, I didn't want to limit my mobility any further. In fact, I wanted to improve it. I was so excited about dancing again that I fantasized about my body becoming more fit and able to do all the physical things I wanted to do. Being strapped to a bed and gaining weight until I couldn't move held zero appeal for me and revealed extremely questionable intentions on the part of the men who wanted to do it. While I loved the security and candidness surrounding food and my body that I reaped while dating a man who liked fat girls, I didn't enjoy the thought of a man physically feeding me. It screamed of infantilism and definitely didn't arouse me. Yes, it was awesome and liberating to feel beautiful and desired in the eyes of a man because of my fat body, but ultimately I didn't want to be solely objectified, either. And I definitely didn't like the tone some of these men adopted when they messaged me, as if they were bestowing the gift of sexual attraction upon me. Having a man say he was mostly interested in my belly was no different than when I was thin and knowing a man was mostly interested in a svelte waistline. Being encouraged to gain weight for a man's sexual pleasure was no different than being asked to lose it for the same reason. I have no problem with men and women mutually engaging in whatever makes them happy—feeding, squashing, gaining—go for it, but it's just not for me.

Was it possible to find a man who valued me wholly and completely, while wanting to have sex with me, too? One whose affections for me wouldn't fluctuate with each pound lost or gained? I wasn't sure, but I wanted to find out.

I was slowly starting to love my body, and I knew my body deserved to be loved. Both my outlook and my goals had begun to shift. I'd spoken so much about my struggles on the radio that identifying myself as a fat woman started to become less scary and shameful. I no longer wanted to achieve my goal weight of 130 pounds. I didn't want my entire life to amount to a weight-loss success story. Losing weight didn't eliminate my anxiety, my self-loathing, or even the way other people treated me. Even after losing 100 pounds, I was still nowhere near what society deemed acceptable.

So if my life wasn't going to be a weight-loss story, what *was* it going to be?

I was desperate to know. I wanted to know what it would feel like to look at myself naked for five minutes and not cry. I wanted to feel love that wasn't conditional.

One day, I was feeling particularly ballsy. I pulled up my T-shirt and tucked it into my sports bra, leaving my stomach exposed. I posted it on my Facebook page with the hashtag #nobodyshamecampaign (which has now been shortened to #nobodyshame) and was bombarded with likes and comments from other people with words of praise, confusion, and even envy. The response was overwhelmingly positive, and I excitedly asked my father if he'd seen the post. His answer broke my heart. He made a strange noise and said, "Well, I don't think that's a very flattering picture."

What ensued was the worst argument I've ever had with my dad. I yelled at him and told him he was like every asshole guy I'd ever met. The next day, when I sat down with him to patch things up, he explained to me that he ultimately wanted me to be happy, but he was worried that if I never lost weight there would be no way to avoid the shitstorm from society.

"I want two things for you: for you to be healthy and live a long life and for you to be happy while you're living it. That's it," he said. "I know you're beautiful. I know you're intelligent. I know how hard you had to work to lose any weight. I know how incredible you are. You're strong; you're a leader; you're capable of accomplishing anything. I've known these things my whole life. But I also know that trying to get the rest of the world to see that isn't going to be easy, and thinking about you being miserable because people are so stupid kills me. *"You're not going to be able to change the world, but you can change yourself,"* he told me.

Having this conversation with my dad was cathartic. I realized that he didn't necessarily care that I was fat—he cared that it was the cause of so much pain and grief in my life, and he just wanted that to be over for me. I understood that he thought changing myself to assimilate into a culture that was unforgiving to fat women would be easier than weathering fat phobia my whole life or somehow single-handedly eradicating it myself. But as much as I understood where he was coming from, I was *done* changing for other people. My father and I both cried, and I promised him that I was going to be fine—that I was feeling stronger than I ever had in my life and that I didn't want him to worry about me. Then I made myself a promise: I would stop caring what people thought about my body and start living in it. I didn't want to waste any more time waiting until I was thin to do things, fall in love, or be happy. I told myself that "I'm fat" could no longer be an excuse to not do something. This resolution to live my life the way I wanted, regardless of my weight, was nothing short of revolutionary for me.

Not only was I starting to love my body, but I was finally starting to love myself. I loved my brain, which mentally corrected every grammatical error in the newspaper and kept me up at night ruminating on existential questions. I loved my personality, which earned me childhood nicknames like the "Energizer Bunny" and got me in trouble for talking too much. I loved my curious spirit that wondered at what was on the other side of the universe. Most important, I also started to accept—and value—my past. I could weep for the one hundred-ninety-pound, fifth-grade Whitney who dodged the "Baby Beluga" song, the middle school Whitney who started throwing up her food, and the college Whitney who battled depression only to be hit with a PCOS diagnosis. I could also let those Whitneys go a little—not completely, as they will always be tethered to me, but I could let them float away on loose strings instead of allowing them to anchor me in shame.

A path had unfolded in front of me and I was sprinting toward it. A better life was waiting for me—I could see it glimmering in my mind like a tiny house on a steep hill—and only I could take the journey there. My life was coming into focus.

My mom was right. *Something good was going to happen.*

9

I DO IT WITH
THE LIGHTS ON

Back in the early spring of 2013, before that huge talk with my dad, before I'd coined "No Body Shame," before I'd been thrust into the online fetish community, and before my mom had given me the pendant on my twenty-ninth birthday, a local photographer named Misty had contacted me to tell me that she was a bigger woman and a radio listener, and that hearing me in the mornings had really helped her build her confidence. As a thank-you, she had offered to give me a free photo shoot. I had never done a legit photo shoot before, and I wasn't entirely certain it was something I wanted to do, but I didn't want to turn down such a nice gift, so I convinced Donna to go with me and we drove out to her studio.

Misty and her crew (made up of her family and friends) were warm and welcoming, but still, purposefully positioning my huge body in front of a camera lens felt uncomfortable. This is exactly what fat women were supposed to avoid, right? With Misty's coaching, I struck a few poses in my pinup-style attire, and when I got the photos back, I didn't hate them, but my immediate thought was: God, I've gotten so fat.

Donna and me at the first photo shoot (2013).

Fast-forward several months to the fall of 2013, and now Misty had offered to do a second photo shoot for me, this time boudoir-style. Coincidentally, I had *just* made the promise to myself about not using hating my body as an excuse to avoid uncomfortable things, so I went through with it. I loved the resulting photos (as you may remember, "Sarah Lynn" hated them). This, of course, was when I fired off that open letter to "Sarah Lynn." I felt more empowered than I ever had in my life. Not only could I see past how fat I was to appreciate the boudoir photos (that's not to say that I didn't see my fat, because, believe me, I did), but the shift in my perspective had finally clicked into place. I felt a strange, buzzing energy.

"I feel like I'm on the cusp of something," I told my mom. The holidays came and went, and at the end of January, I was still living my daily radio grind, fantasizing about the day when I would be able to afford rent again and could move out of my parents' house.

I was driving around downtown when I heard a snippet of a new song on the radio that I loved. I hadn't caught much of the lyrics, but the beat was infectious. When I got to work, I searched the daily log to find out what song it was, then went to my office to Google it. It was called "Talk Dirty" by Jason Derulo, and when I popped the title into my Web browser, a dance tutorial came up. The choreographer was an Australian dancer named Jasmin Meakin, and she was fabulous. Then I saw that an in-depth tutorial was available for purchase online. I thought it would make a great Fat Girl Dancing video, so I downloaded it and began learning it right then and there in my cramped office.

The choreography was fast and too difficult for me in spots. By the time I called Todd and asked him to meet me at the Y, I'd already modified it, "fat girl style," to suit me. Todd was in town only for a couple days, and he hadn't yet made an official Fat Girl Dancing appearance since I'd started making the videos for the radio station. I taught him the choreography over two days, and on the second, I brought my laptop in to record it. Because we were pressed for time (Todd was about to head back to NYC, where he lived at the time) and not at all performance-ready, we danced the choreography over and over, always messing up so badly that it couldn't be used from start to finish. When I got home later that evening, sweaty and exhausted, I had multiple videos to choose from, so I spliced the best two routines together and called it a night.

The next day, like I had done with all my Fat Girl Dancing videos before, I uploaded it to our station's Facebook page. But I soon noticed that something was different. The video was getting more shares and comments than anything we'd ever posted. Every time I logged in to social media, I saw it posted somewhere else, and the most surprising thing was that every person who reposted it did so in a congratulatory way—I never saw people sharing it to make fun of me (that, of course, is what comment sections are for). After a few days, I had collected over 100K followers.

I was at work over the weekend, sitting in my office, and every time I refreshed the video, I could see the views jumping by tens of thousands. I called my dad and asked him to come over. I showed him the video, the views, and some of the feedback I was getting. He seemed marginally interested, but I don't think he thought it was that wild.

"Dad, seriously, something is happening," I told him, showing him how the views kept piling up. "What is happening?"

It's a strange feeling to describe, but at that moment, something was set into motion. I could *feel,* almost tangibly, my life changing from minute to minute. It's a sensation I've never felt before and probably will never feel again.

The next day I got an email from *The Huffington Post,* saying they wanted to publish a story about the video. I was shocked and honored, and I believed, hands-down, that this was the biggest thing that would ever happen to me in my entire life.

But it didn't stop with *The Huffington Post.* They asked me to post the video on YouTube so that they would have an embeddable link, and I did so. That YouTube video immediately attracted millions of views and now has almost nine million. After the HuffPo piece ran, I got a phone call from a strange number on my cellphone. It was a producer from *Inside Edition* who said they wanted to fly out to North Carolina to shoot an interview with me. I said yes, but the next day when the interview was scheduled, I got a call saying they had to cancel it. I was a little disappointed but, wow, what a fun ride, I thought. I thought this would forever be the pinnacle of my life.

The next day, I was at a stoplight checking my email. I had a message from a producer on the *Steve Harvey* show, asking me if I wanted to be a guest. I had to pull over on the side of the road. The day after, the *Today* show called. An hour after that, *Good Morning America.* An hour after *that,* I had a panic attack.

A friend of mine, who witnessed my anxiety, told me she knew a great agent in town named Michael and that I should call him. I dialed his number and he asked me what was going on, and so I told him. Not just that I had a viral video and some national press requests, but I told him *everything*.

Speaking quickly and excitedly, I tried to explain this crazy, surreal, wonderful thing that was coming together. It was more than a dance video; *it was the culmination of my entire life*. It was the decades of strife and self-hate. It was the realization that fat-hate was universal. It was the difficult truth that losing weight hadn't fixed my problems. It was the way dance had wrapped me back up in its arms, without punishing me for leaving for so long. It was the joy of meeting my soul sister, Donna; the comfort of my oldest friend, Heather; and the steadfast companion-ship of Todd, Tal, Buddy, and Ashley, who'd loved me through thick and thin. It was the sneak peek into the fetish world and a glimpse into territory I didn't know existed—a place where fat women were beautiful. It was me choosing to have my picture taken without cropping my body out, and even more, the im-pulsive decision to hashtag a photo in which I'm baring my en-tire belly and feeling good about it with #nobodyshame. It was fighting through loneliness and depression when I felt like my life was going nowhere, and ultimately deciding that I never had to be skinny again to be okay. It was the absolute unconditional love of parents who never failed me, and the ease with which I trusted Misty to photograph me without a shirt on. And mostly, it was the strength I found somewhere inside me to respond to criticism, because I finally felt like I had become the author of my own story. It was my voice that I was finally unafraid to use—and that I demanded be heard.

If Michael was overwhelmed by our two-hour phone conver-sation, he didn't let on. Instead, he got right to work for me, negotiating appearances and booking meetings. I jumped on a plane to Chicago to film a segment for *Steve Harvey* that would air two weeks later. My appearance would include a sit-down interview with Steve followed by a dance performance that, unbeknownst to him, would transform into a flash mob with the studio audience. When I walked into the hair and makeup room, the stylist shrieked.

"Oh my God! I just saw you on the Internet! You're the dancer, right?"

"Yes," I replied, breaking out into a smile. Then I gave myself permission to say it: *"I'm the dancer."*

Minutes before I met Steve, I called my parents backstage, and my dad echoed the message he'd instilled in me since childhood: "You're gonna do it, girl. You can do anything you put your mind to." Twenty minutes later, during a pause in the filming, Steve leaned over the arm of his white leather chair and locked eyes with me. "You've got good energy," he said. "Real good energy."

An hour later, with the interview, dance, and flash mob all done, I was whisked out of a loading-dock door and into a limo with fluorescent, strobing lights. On the way to the airport a hard rain began to fall. I pulled out my cellphone and wrote a text to my brother with shaky fingers. *Steve Harvey said I had good energy!!!!!!!*

When I got back to Greensboro, I barely had time to think before I prepared for my next appearance. This one was for the *Today* show, and it would be live, so it would be the first time a national audience would see me on TV. My mom, dad, and my manager, Michael, all flew up to New York with me. I sat in my hotel room that evening, scrolling through hundreds of posts on Facebook. I had solicited for people to send me their selfies using #nobodyshame and I was speechless at the hundreds that had poured in. As I clicked through them, I saw colorful photos of women, men, and children of different races, shapes, sizes, and ages—all of them proud to use the hashtag. The viral Fat Girl Dancing video had led to all this new media attention, but everyone kept asking: what is No Body Shame? To put it simply, I decided that the message of No Body Shame was this: Love yourself. Live fully. No excuses. No shame. It was a lifestyle I had just begun living when my dance video serendipitously went viral, and here I was, about to go on live national television to talk about a concept, "body-positivity," that I'd never even heard of a month before. The fortuitous nature of it all was almost too much to handle.

I woke up early the next morning filled with jitters. When I got outside to the street, I called my parents and asked them to come meet me. A few minutes later I saw not only Mom and Dad, but my brother, too! He'd been living in New York since 2005, but I didn't expect him to accompany us to the *Today* show appearance. We hugged tighter than we ever had before. "You're such a bad-ass," he whispered in my ear. I was so overwhelmed with love and excitement and nerves that I could hardly stand it. A couple hours later, when my interview began, I could see my parents, my brother, and Michael standing offstage just feet away from where I was sitting with Kathie Lee and Hoda. After the interview, I did a dance segment in the Orange Room, walked in a fashion show segment, and met *American Idol* winner Jordin Sparks, who was dating Jason Derulo (the artist who sang the song I danced to in my viral video). "Ahhh!" she'd yelled. "I shared that video!" When the thrilling morning was over, Mom, Dad, Hunter, Michael, and I took the short walk back to our hotel. My mom was so caught up in the excitement of the day and so proud of me that after covering me in kisses, she almost passed out (Michael caught her). Before we headed upstairs to our room, my dad pulled me aside, squinting in the midmorning sunlight.

"I couldn't believe it, girl," he started. "You were incredible. Unbelievable. I was watching you up there thinking, 'Is this my daughter? Can this really be my daughter?'" Then his voice broke, and I saw tears wet his eyes. "I know I told you that you couldn't change the world," he said, "but, by God, if you aren't changing it." Then he paused. "I was wrong."

Within a couple months, I'd appeared live on *Steve Harvey, Today, Good Morning America, Huffington Post Live, Inside Edition, CNN Headline News,* and *Right This Minute,* as well as given dozens of phone and Skype interviews here and abroad. There had been articles in *Cosmopolitan* and *Vanity Fair Italia. Woman's Day* named me one of "Ten Women Who Are Changing the Face of Beauty."

As soon as I got back from my press tour, I contemplated what I would do next. I was still holding down my radio job, but I was majorly distracted. No Body Shame wasn't something I could keep leaving work for—I strongly felt that it *was* my work.

Then I received another crazy email. This one was from the TLC TV network, and I fished it out of my spam box. It was a simple, three-sentence email saying that they had seen me on the *Today* show and were wondering if I'd consider collaborating with them on a project. I didn't really know what that meant, but I said yes. I scheduled a meeting with a representative in New York, and after that they told me there was a long process ahead—they would have to find a production company to film a sizzle reel, and then the network would decide what they wanted to do with it. This could be anything, from saying "Thanks, but no thanks" to ordering a pilot and ordering episodes. It was March, and I wouldn't hear anything about even meeting the production company until summer, but somehow I just knew inside me that my time in radio was done and there was something else in store. But, I should point out, I didn't think a reality show was it. It seemed too implausible that such a huge opportunity would come to fruition. Plus, I wasn't at all sold on doing reality TV to begin with.

Even though I was still broke and living with my parents, I

decided to quit my job at the radio station and turn all my attention to No Body Shame. I was still regularly fielding interview requests and invitations both here and abroad, and there seemed to be no indication it would be slowing down anytime soon. I sat at my computer for hours each day, responding to the thousands of people who sent me messages and emails.

Reading these messages filled me with a strange feeling of both happiness and sadness, because what I found was this: people all over the world, regardless of race, gender, orientation, ability, size ... they were all struggling, and so many of their stories mirrored my own. I was not unique, and it was tragic because I couldn't believe how commonplace my depression and pain were for other people. I'd wished that it wasn't as "normal" as I was learning it was. But then I realized something else. If I am not unique, then I am not alone. *None of us is alone.* I drew strength from the gay boy in Lebanon who told me that watching my dance video gave him courage because being gay is a crime where he lives. I felt for the thousands of young girls, some of whom had been diagnosed with PCOS like me, and had, for too long, let their weight stop them from living the lives they wanted. I could sympathize with every person who wrote to me about suffering from a skin condition, a physical disability, or who was just plain critical of their own reflection.

In the summer TLC scheduled me a meeting with a production company called Pilgrim. When I had told my mom that we might be doing reality TV, her only response was, "Whitney, I'm not doing it." But the more *I* thought about it, the more optimistic I became. Of course, agreeing to let cameras into your home and personal space was absurd, but I thought the list of pros outweighed the cons. I had never seen a TV show that centered around a fat woman in a positive way, and neither had the thousands of young, miserable girls who wrote to me. I had never heard PCOS being discussed on a national scale. I knew that agreeing to do a reality show could be the worst or the best decision of my life, but after considering all the possibilities (it could be awesome, it could get canceled after an episode, it could tarnish my reputation, it could be fun, it could effectively squash any future job opportunities and ruin my life, etc.), I got on a plane and agreed to go to Los Angeles for the meeting with Pilgrim. I was nervous as all hell, and had spent two hours in my hotel room getting ready, only to end up with smudged eyeliner and sweat stains on my clothes. When I sat down in a huge conference room with a long table in the middle, I looked up at the walls and saw framed titles of all of their previous successful shows. When a producer walked in, he said, "Hopefully you'll be up there one day soon." The thought of it made my stomach turn. It's not every day you go from being a normal person to having a worldwide audience overnight, and then get handed a television show. It seemed more like a movie than my real life.

When the meeting started, it was casual. I was hyperaware of trying to just "act natural" and be myself, because that is what they liked, after all. The producer asked, "What are your short-term goals?"

For some reason, in that moment, I lost all ability to think of anything, much less articulate it, and before I knew it I had opened up my mouth and said, "Well, I'd really like to get laid, for starters!" Oh *GOD!* Had I really just said that? I envisioned my mom clutching her pearls, and me getting on the plane downtrodden, shaking my head, wondering how I had ruined it all.

But then everyone burst into laughter. When the meeting was over, the producer said, "You're the most positive person I've ever met." I smiled and thanked him, and when I got into my car to head back to the hotel, I noticed a missed call from him. I listened to my voicemail and he said that it was nice to meet me and that he'd just booked me three nights in Vegas. The meeting had gone well.

A month or so later a crew came out to film for a few days, to gather material to make a sizzle reel. They filmed my normal life—talking to my parents, hanging out with my friends, dancing in the studio with Todd—and when they left, I wondered what on earth they were going to do with the footage to make it something anyone would want to watch on TV. But then a month after that I got a phone call from the same TLC executive who had emailed me after seeing me on the *Today* show.

"Do you want to be on TV in January of next year?" she asked.

Um, duh!

And just like that I suddenly became a person with her own TV show. I couldn't wait for the next month, when production would start. When the crew arrived in Greensboro, any fears my family and I had about reality TV were quelled. They were normal, wonderful people whom we grew to love over the next three months as we shot enough material for nine episodes. When they left at the beginning of November to go back to California, I missed them.

Now that I was waiting for season one of *My Big Fat Fabulous Life* to premiere (and I couldn't even talk about it until people.com broke the story in December!), and I didn't have much of a daily schedule, I was just plain bored. I signed up for a new dating app called Tinder and crossed my fingers. Surprisingly enough, I matched with a handsome guy named Peter and we started chatting right away. Then we exchanged numbers and continued our conversation. After a few days he suggested meeting. I took my new kitten to meet Boo Boo for an ice cream cone on a nearby college campus. We sat at the picnic table outside, my kitten's tiny head poking out of my sports bra, and she read all the text messages from Peter.

"Boo Boo," Donna said, "he sounds so normal. I really think you have to meet him. What can you lose?"

"Besides my dignity?" I joked, but I softened a little. She was right: Peter was the first "normal" guy to come along in a while. I also realized that my standards of "normal" were pretty lenient. That is to say, he was smart, spoke to me respectfully, wrote in full sentences, and had a sense of humor. He'd never been crude, he'd never suggested Netflix and Chill, and he appeared to have substance. What made him different from the last few guys I'd dated was that he wasn't exclusively into fat girls, and in fact had never been with a fat girl at all.

"It's more about lack of opportunity than preference," Peter had explained. "I do think I'm generally attracted to thinner women, but an attractive woman is an attractive woman." I didn't fault him for preferring thin women, nor did I think it was a deal breaker that he'd never pursued a bigger one, but the thought of being someone's "first" felt like so much pressure. Still, the more I hashed it out with Donna, the more I felt I had nothing to lose. I wasn't looking to fall in love or meet my soulmate; I just wanted some company. This dude had no bearing on my life, my self-worth, or my achievements. I should meet him.

A few nights later, while Donna was over, Peter and I were texting intermittently, when I broached meeting up in person.

Right now? he texted.

"Oh God! He meant right now!" I said to Boo Boo, holding up my phone so she could see the screen.

"Say yes!" Donna jumped off the bed and started gathering dirty clothes from my floor. "Get in the shower. Your room will be clean when you get out. Do you need anything? I can run to the store."

I hopped in the shower while Donna filled hampers with

clothes, made my bed, replaced the empty spaces on my shelves with books from various spots in my room, and lit a candle. As I blow-dried my hair, I had only minutes remaining before Peter was supposed to show up. I asked Donna to stay until he got there, and when there was a soft knock at my parents' back door, we both went into the hallway. I let Peter in, and Donna—ever the wing woman—offered to get us Popsicles from the kitchen. Then she gave me a hug and left.

For all the anticipation of impending doom I'd thought up in my brain, the evening was totally normal. Peter *was* smart and funny and all the things I picked up on via text. We kissed before he left. We had sushi the day after that, followed by another week of serious make-out sessions. He was cool; it felt easy.

But when Peter invited me over to his place for the first time, I felt a little out of control. I hurried down the walkway in the cold and reached his building. I took the stairs as fast as I could, and when I got to the top I was a little out of breath. I paused, listening to his voice from outside his door, inhaling and exhaling slowly so I wouldn't appear winded.

What am I doing? I thought. Who cares if you look a little out of breath! You just flew up the stairs! As a fat woman, I am acutely aware of stairs, hills, and other "complications" when I am in mixed company. Call it leftover insecurity or too much pride, but I struggle with accepting that I am incapable of doing everything a fit person can do. Around my close friends, of course, this is not a problem. So what was Peter? A friend who I wanted to have sex with? Did that mean I could unzip my insecurity? I wasn't sure.

When I entered his apartment, I saw another obstacle. Peter's friend was sitting on the one small couch and Peter was in an armchair. I am horrible at estimating how much space my body takes up, and I notoriously underestimate my size. I can't tell you how many times I've tried to shimmy between two parked cars only to almost take someone's rearview mirror clean off.

Conversely, there have been plenty of times I take the long way around in a restaurant only to realize I could have maneuvered through the open space easily.

I couldn't tell if I would take up more than my half of Peter's couch, but when it comes to seating arrangements, surface area is only half the battle. I can tell, simply by looking, if a couch or chair will swallow me up, leaving me leaning far backward, feet almost off the floor with my boobs nearly suffocating me. To get off of this type of couch, I have to grab the armrest and first wiggle to the end before my feet can touch and then I can stand up. I call this move "walrusing." Because of all of this hassle, I routinely sit on the edge of couches and chairs so my back never goes near the back of the furniture. That way I can remain upright, assertive, in control, and non-walrus. Being in the intimate space of a man who I wanted to be sleeping with heightened my anxiety. But instead of letting it devour me, I simply motioned to the chair.

"Would you mind if I sat there?"

Peter immediately got up and joined his friend on the couch, none the wiser to my concerns. This might seem like a simple thing, but it's something I'd been working on for a long time. In my quest to never be specially accommodated because of my size, I had either quit going places or suffered in silence in full-out walrus. Part of my journey in body-positivity has been about becoming able to ask for simple things that made my body more comfortable, instead of feeling ashamed of how much space my body takes up. We talked and laughed, watched YouTube videos and played Heads Up on my phone. Peter's friend eventually left and I stretched out on the couch. Peter walked over to me.

He bent down and put his mouth on mine, his curly hair dangling on my cheek.

"Come on," he said.

"Come on where?"

"To the bedroom."

He didn't have to tell me twice. I was off the couch in a second (imagine that), but when I got to the door of the bedroom, I stopped, almost afraid to go in because of what I saw. He was in the process of buying a new bed, and all he had was an air mattress on the hardwood floor.

"Is that . . . an air mattress?" I squeaked.

"Yeah. What's wrong?"

"Don't those things have a weight limit?"

He laughed. "I'm sure you'll be fine. Come on."

"But what if . . . what if I break it?"

Hearing myself have this conversation out loud was shocking, even to me. With any other man, at any other time in my life, I would have run at the sight of that air mattress. But here I was, calmly explaining my concerns about bursting this man's twin air mattress during the sex I felt sure we were going to have, and he wasn't budging.

"Whitney. Come on."

Even lowering my body to get on the air mattress was awkward, as it was only four inches off the floor, but I made it down. "If something horrible happens, please let me replace it."

"Deal," he said as he pulled me out of my shirt.

He kissed me with the passion of a man who had loved me for lifetimes, expertly covering every inch of my body. And he listened, not to what I was saying out loud (which wasn't much besides breathless gasps), but he intuitively listened to my body. Even more surprising: though my body was at least twice the size of his, we maneuvered together with ease. One minute he was on top of me and the next I was on my knees with no real memory of how I got there. There was no awkwardness, no changing of positions, and no time for me to worry about what my body looked like from his perspective. There was only pleasure. As I lay there on my side, processing what had just happened—on an air mattress, no less—I looked over at the lamp on the floor and did something I'd never done once with my boyfriends in the twelve years I'd been having sex. I turned the light *off*. We even both managed to lie side by side and cuddle afterward.

"I don't think I can sleep over at your house," I said with a laugh.

"Probably not the best idea if either of us want to get any sleep," he agreed.

I said goodbye and made my way back to my car. As I drove home, I replayed the events in my mind and thought about the freedom I'd felt during our encounter. And I felt really proud of myself. Here's why: before my fling with Peter, I'd always thought that having sex with the lights on, completely unencumbered by insecurity or body image issues, was something a man *gave* you. I thought this kind of sex, which I'd only read about and seemed as common as a unicorn, must exist only within the four walls of a bedroom that belonged to a man who (1) loved you, (2) was in a monogamous relationship with you, and (3) had more or less taught you to love your body because, by some crazy fluke, he did.

I figured a man would have to systematically break down your walls, steadfastly chiseling away at your self-doubt and in-hibition, kind of like fashioning a beautiful ice sculpture out of a glacier—it was only the *right man* who could make you into the kind of woman who had sex with the lights on. The right man would be equal parts understanding and encouraging. It was the kind of narrative rom-coms had fed me, and until this night I had wholly bought into it. But here I was, without the right man, doing it with the lights on. So why now? Why Peter? Why on an air mattress?

By the time I reached my house, I had the answer. It was be-cause of me. *I* had changed. Sure, Peter was a nice guy, and I needed a little coaxing with the mattress, but the confidence and the comfort weren't something a man had taught me to have or feel; they had come, genuinely, from inside of me. I liked

Peter a lot, but I didn't love him. We were on the same page there. And so, after many years of chasing this elusive satisfying sex life, I found it precisely when I didn't expect to. It turns out that I didn't need relationship security; I didn't need a Superman to play the role of therapist while he got me out of my pants. I just needed peace. Peace with my body, peace with myself, peace with the notion that I—even in all my imperfections—deserved good sex.

It was the beginning of January, just days before the premiere of *My Big Fat Fabulous Life,* and my family and Tal and I were in Pasadena at TCA. The Television Critics Association conference is a twice-yearly event where critics watch clips from upcoming series and have the opportunity to ask questions of the guests and interview them. We were asked by TLC to attend, as *My Big Fat Fabulous Life* was the show the network would be presenting to the critics. I, of course, had not seen the show. I was only privy to the same short clip as the rest of the world and prepared to answer the same questions my existence usually prompted, such as, "Aren't you promoting obesity?"

The TCA panel went smoothly, and I was shocked at the softball nature of the questions. Not one journalist questioned whether I was promoting obesity (still curious? Read chapter 11!), but plenty of them were interested in talking to me afterward. As I did the rounds of AP, *Entertainment Tonight,* and *Inside Edition,* I was struck by how people seemed to connect to my story, whether it was a perfectly coiffed woman who resembled a Barbie doll or the middle-aged man who approached my dad to tell him he really identified with my struggle. My family left California excited about the upcoming premiere, and I got on a plane to Chicago to kick off another press tour, which included a second appearance on *Today, Steve Harvey,* and *CNN Headline*

News, as well as an appearance on *Dr. Oz* and a host of magazine interviews and phone calls.

My flight home was scheduled to land just an hour before the first episode of *My Big Fat Fabulous Life* would premiere, and my parents and friends were waiting for me at the restaurant where we were having a party.

As we sat on the tarmac, waiting to take off, my stomach filled up with butterflies. It seemed like an eon ago that I was told I was getting a show, and ages since we'd filmed it. It was hard to believe that it was real. I opened up Facebook and saw a post from my alma mater, Appalachian State University, congratulating me and announcing the premiere. As I scrolled through the comments, I saw people mostly talking shit, groaning about how awful it was to be associated with such a fat bitch. Just as I was about to close the app, I noticed a comment from an old roommate whom I'd not heard from in eight years.

I know this girl, she wrote. *I lived with her. She's a disgusting fat slob who did nothing but stuff her face all day long. I can't believe she graduated!* Seeing the name and (false) sentiments of this girl whom I couldn't stand to begin with filled me with rage. And I couldn't believe she still despised me so many years later. But it was a lesson I needed to learn. Some people are deeply committed to hating me, and by extension, my ideals and contributions. I couldn't waste any time on people like her, I told myself, but I was still afraid that more of the same would be directed my way by the end of the night.

When I pulled into the parking lot of the restaurant two hours later, Buddy, Boo Boo, and Heather met me outside. We were all overflowing with nervous energy and giddy to the gills. They led me inside, where my dad, true to form, was giving a speech to the hundred people in attendance.

"I don't really know what to say," I stammered. "I have so many feelings that I can't name because I have absolutely no context for this situation, but thank you so much for supporting me and for being here." Within minutes a glass of champagne was shoved in my hand and we were all seated to watch the show.

All the nervousness I'd had about it was gone in an instant. That was me on the screen! I looked like me. I sounded like me. There was Todd! My mother was hilarious!

"Why is this the funniest show on TV?" Heather shouted.

"I don't know!" I yelled back through happy tears.

I went to the bathroom and called my brother, who was watching the show during work while he bartended.

"Hunter!" I said when he picked up. And then we both just screamed.

Watching My Big Fat Fabulous Life *for the first time! (2015).*

With all the people I love the most at the premiere party for My Big Fat Fabulous Life *(2015).*

I learned the next day that 1.3 million people had tuned in to the premiere of my show in the United States. By the time four episodes had aired, we were renewed for season two. A month later I went to London for the premiere of the show, called *Whitney: Fat Girl Dancing* in the UK. When I arrived in my posh Covent Garden hotel room, I was hit with a wave of gratitude. What was my life becoming? Was that genuine Frida Kahlo art on the walls? How had I gotten so lucky?

I visited the BBC for an interview, as well as a morning program called *Lorraine* (the British Oprah, I'm told). Both of them were how all my interviews had always been: upbeat and positive. But the next day I endured a horrific interview by Eamonn Holmes on *Sky News*. I was scheduled to appear on the program to discuss the premiere, and the producer prepped me for the same kind of interview I'd been giving for a year. I would explain how my Fat Girl Dancing videos led to a TV show and what I hoped the show would accomplish: to portray the life of a fat woman who is neither miserable nor specifically on a weight-loss journey, humanizing other fat people along the way. But as soon as the cameras started rolling on the live interview, it was nothing like what I had expected.

"Some people at home, they see you and you're dancing, but they might be saying, 'Who're you kidding?' Do you really think this is the kind of advertisement you should be giving to young people?"

It was only eight A.M. and I was jet-lagged, but I knew my message backward and forward. It's not something I needed to be coached on, and no media training could prepare me more than my own experiences. While I was shocked at Eamonn's line of questioning, I handled it with grace and ease, remaining positive and assertive throughout. Eamonn tried to couch his questions by pointing out that his own weight is often ridiculed in the media. When it was over, and I watched it, the title at the bottom of the screen didn't say anything about my show but instead read, *Obesity Debate* and *Big, Fat, and Fabulous?* Question mark. My PR person was horrified and apologized over and over. I told her it was okay but that it had caught me off guard since that was in no way the kind of interview I had prepped for. I was a little shaken. Shortly afterward, *Huffington Post UK* published an article titled, "Whitney Thore Hits Back in Obesity Debate."

More than a year later I saw Eamonn Holmes interviewing Megan, one of my British friends in the body-positive community, whom I'd met through Instagram. Recovered from anorexia, Megan is conventionally beautiful and amazing, and every bit as radical as I am in her commitment to unapologetic self-love, but Eamonn treated us completely differently. He was sympathetic to Megan throughout her interview and made several inappropriate comments about how attractive he found her, while she was—get this—dancing in her underwear, for the express purpose of celebrating how her fat jiggled. So basically, doing the exact same thing that I do on the Internet but with fewer articles of clothing. Eamonn's hypocrisy was maddening.

When I got back to the U.S., I traveled to New York to appear on *The View*. My brother met me there and he stayed in my dressing room while I went to Hair and Makeup. I thought about how happy I was to be able to spend time with Hunter and how much our relationship had grown once I'd started loving myself. I've always told Hunter that he was my hero and we were becoming closer than we'd ever been as adults. As I was getting my hair curled, Whoopi Goldberg came in and casually sat in the chair beside me. Oh my God! I thought. Seriously, what is my life right now? It was Rosie O'Donnell's last day hosting, and she greeted me enthusiastically, telling me her best friend was a big fan. Rosie asked if I would make her a video, and of course I obliged. She held my hands in hers and told me about her weight-loss surgery and how it changed her life. She asked her assistant to give me her card and said that if I wanted to talk to her doctor or needed any help, to call her. I told her that I wasn't particularly interested in weight-loss surgery but I appreciated her kindness and perspective. When the interview was over, Hunter met me offstage for a hug. "I know you always say that I'm your hero, but honestly, you're mine," he said.

When all the whirlwind press died down and I was back in North Carolina gearing up to shoot season two of *My Big Fat Fabulous Life*, I decided to pass the time by swiping on Tinder some more. I'd met Peter there, after all. Late at night, in the darkness of my room, I came across a picture of a man with a huge beard and soft blue eyes holding a small Pomeranian. His Instagram handle was in his description, so I looked him up. His name was Lennie. He was an artist. I swiped right and saw immediately that we matched. Feeling ballsy, I messaged him straightaway. To avoid being too basic and mentioning his beard, as I'm sure every girl did, I tried a different approach.

I enjoy both your dog and your art, I typed.

He wrote back immediately, telling me he knew Buddy, so he'd heard of me. When the small talk petered out, I went to bed. The next day I'd all but forgotten about the exchange until a new Tinder message popped up.

I should draw you some body-positive animals saying puns. Like a beaver looking into a river saying, "Dam, I look good."

This impressed me on multiple levels. He'd obviously done some homework on me. His mention of body-positivity let me know he was clued in to the most important thing in my life. And how had he found out I loved beavers? We exchanged numbers. Later that day a new number appeared on my phone.

Hi Whitney! It's Lennie from Tinder.

Naturally, the thought crossed my mind that Lennie was texting simply to offer to give me artwork because he wanted me to share it with my considerable social network. It certainly would not have been the first time, so I was wary of his intentions. I tested the waters.

How much are you charging for the body-pos animals bringing the life-affirming puns? I inquired.

I'm not sure, he answered. *Want to get together and discuss it?*

Lennie planned a painting date for us a few days later. I consulted Peter, who was now just a friend. He was dubious.

It sounds like he could just want you to hock his artwork.

Yeah, you're probably right, I agreed. *I guess we'll see!*

The next evening, as I got ready, I incessantly texted Peter photos, out of nervousness. Before shower. Midshower. After shower. After makeup. After blow-drying my hair.

Whoa. 8 texts in a row. Haha, he wrote. And then: *Gorgeous. Slay, babe.*

When Lennie and I met in person forty-five minutes later, we gave each other a nervous hug. We had barely had one conversation, and I'd never met someone from the Internet so soon. But I wasn't in the business of wasting any time with these things. Lennie was on the quiet side, but conversation flowed naturally. At some point he laughed and said, "This is the best date I've ever been on."

"So it is a date?" I teased playfully.

"Yeah, of course it is."

The next day, he came over and brought me a small framed sketch of a vibrant butterfly with outstretched wings and a caption that read, *Fuck, I'm beautiful.* I recognized it because I'd liked a photo of it on his Instagram. Two weeks later, with all the ease and self-assurance in the world, I asked him to be my boyfriend.

And yes, after *that,* Lennie and I would have sex with the lights on. But I'd end up falling in love with him first.

10

FEMINISM IS MY
FAVORITE F-WORD

On Valentine's Day last year *Cosmo* published an article about me titled, "'Fat Girl Dancing' Whitney Thore Wants to Find a 'Delicious, Feminist Man.'" Farther down in the article, I elaborate on what I'm looking for in a partner, saying, "Someone who is intelligent on a bigger scale, not just book-smart, but I need someone who thinks about life really critically. I need a man who is an unapologetic feminist. If he's not, it's just not going to work, and I need a guy that can make me laugh. I do love a beard, too, love a little tattoo or a piercing and all that. The physical attributes could be a lot of different things, but definitely I need a smart, critically thinking, open-minded, feminist, delicious man."

In order to talk about feminism, and why it is so momentously important for every human being on this planet, we first have to get the definition straight. If you've listened to Beyoncé's song "Flawless," you're already ahead of the game. As the voice of Chimamanda Ngozi Adichie defines over the top of the music, "Feminist: a person who believes in the social, economic, and political equality of the sexes." Of course, we could have consulted good ol' *Merriam-Webster's* for that clarification, but isn't everything more fun with Beyoncé? (Answer: Yes. Duh.) So, from here on out, you must abandon all notions that feminists desire to rule over men, overtake them, or otherwise threaten, harm, or humiliate them, and instead operate with full understanding of the textbook definition that describes a simple wish for equality.

Having Lennie—a handsome, intelligent, bearded feminist artist—practically fall into my lap from Tinder, of all places, was surprising. And, based on the majority of my other Tinder experiences, I'm gonna venture to say it's highly unlikely. The incredible truth is that Lennie must have read my *Cosmo* article and thought, "Hey, that's ME!" and set out to find me, because he fits all my "requirements" to a T.

Now, it's easy to understand why I want an *intelligent* man: so we can have thought-provoking discussions and he can help me do simple math problems without my calculator. (Naturally, Lennie has to overachieve; he's in Mensa, for crying out loud!) No one would question why I wanted a man who could *make me laugh,* because laughing is *fun,* and it's completely understandable that *critically thinking* and *open-minded* would make the list, because it's 2016 and that's what we do here. And *delicious*? That's a given. Who doesn't want that? But still, there's the pesky issue of *feminism.* Fine, I'm a feminist, but why does my boyfriend have to be?

A-ha! Perhaps the single most common misunderstanding about feminism, apart from its literal definition, is that it's intended solely for women. This couldn't be further from the truth, because, I assure you, the patriarchy (a system of society or government in which men hold the power and women are largely excluded from it) harms both girls and boys who grow into women and men with deeply rooted beliefs resulting from this system, who then go on to perpetuate it, and . . . you get it, the cycle continues. To eradicate this system and replace it with a more equal one, we need the unequivocal support of both sexes. "But wait," you might say, "women have opportunities, right? What's the holdup and why do I have to care?" Yes, women can vote (in the United States), and yes, women can technically apply for any job they want (in the United States), and sure, rape is a crime (in the United States), but things aren't as rosy as they may seem.

Take a quick peek at these statistics: Did you know that in just about every state in the country, millennial women are more likely than millennial men to have a college degree, yet millennial women also have higher poverty rates and lower earnings than millennial men? Or that it's likely that we won't see equal pay for American women within our lifetime?[*] Or how about the fact that one out of every six American women has been the victim of an attempted or completed rape in her lifetime?[†] The need for inclusive feminism goes even further: Latina women make only 54 percent of what white men make,[‡] 83 percent of women with disabilities will be sexually assaulted in their lifetimes,[§] and black (and other women of color) are routinely characterized as angrier than their white counterparts. (May I remind you of the whole Taylor Swift–Nicki Minaj–Miley Cyrus VMA debacle?)

And, again, this is only in the United States. If you think the patriarchy isn't alive and well, you need to think again—and start being a feminist ally so we can smash it together!

A while back I was scrolling through Instagram when I got a

[*] www.huffingtonpost.com/ariel-smilowitz/for-us-women-inequality-takes-many-forms_b_7064348.html

[†] rainn.org/get-information/statistics/sexual-assault-victims

[‡] www.aauw.org/research/the-simple-truth-about-the-gender-pay-gap

[§] Liz Stimpson and Margaret C. Best, *Courage Above All: Sexual Assault Against Women with Disabilities* (Toronto: Disabled Women's Network, 1991).

notification that I'd been tagged in a photo. When I clicked on it, my screen directed me to an image of a simple line graph, with "body weight" written vertically and "chances she's a feminist" written horizontally. The red line showed an upward trend: the fatter a woman is, the more likely she is to be a feminist. There are plenty of offensive memes of some overweight, "unattractive" (by societal standards) woman wearing a *This Is What a Feminist Looks Like* T-shirt. Naturally, whoever tagged me in this—likely an Internet troll—intended for it to insult me, but all I could think initially was, "Well, you're not completely wrong . . ." Pause. I am NOT reinforcing the belief that feminists are simply embittered ugly women in whom men have no interest (a shockingly common misconception), but I AM saying that my pilgrimage to the holy land of feminism *was* largely influenced by my weight. Lemme break down why.

Even back in high school, when I inhabited a conventionally attractive body, I still had a hint of feminism in me. I was always an independent thinker and I loathed what we now affectionately call "fuck boys." I wrote a long letter to the editor of the school newspaper, calling out my school administration for punishing me for not wearing a bra. I felt empowered; my parents felt embarrassed. But it wasn't until I gained weight that the spark of feminism took hold.

I have a lot of conservative middle-American fans struggling with their weight who blow sunshine and roses up my ass until the minute I mention being a feminist, and then WWIII kicks off. Cue all the comments from women saying things like, "I'm not a feminist, but . . ." and, "I'm so disappointed in you. Why do you hate men?" and, "Whitney, just because you can't find a man doesn't mean you have to hate them," and one of my favorites (and by favorite I mean my least favorite), "I don't believe in feminism. I believe in humanism." Now cue the fathers of actual humanism rolling over in their graves. I'm always flabbergasted at women who seek out the body-positive movement only to renounce feminism in the process.

I've heard many people ask what feminism and "fat acceptance" have to do with each other. For my purposes, let's say "fat acceptance" means that even people who exist in fat bodies or bodies that are not conventionally attractive still deserve basic human respect from others and that these bodies do not strip them of the right to feel worthy, valuable, or beautiful.

As a teenager, I wasn't blind to the systematic sexualization of women in advertising, television, movies, and even in my real life, but I wasn't as concerned with it because it was a system that mostly benefited me. A young, privileged girl submits to the system by offering up her appearance as collateral, and she receives positive attention and affirmation in return for her willingness to play the game. As long as she stays obsessed with her appearance, making it a top priority, society will cheer her on for this and dole out validation accordingly.

I didn't realize at the time that fixating on my weight and appearance was a losing game, of course. No woman is ever thin enough, curvy enough, made-up enough, fresh-faced enough, innocent enough, or provocative enough, depending on what is trendy at any given time. Did you get that? Women's bodies are *trends*—with one body type or aesthetic being dismissed in favor of another, over and over and over again. It's a lose-lose situation that holds women to impossible standards and keeps them forever chasing their "best selves."

When I was conventionally attractive, sure, guys labeled me a slut or turned around to call me fat if I rejected their advances, but they were still interested in me in one way or another. I had something they wanted, and that made me feel valuable to some degree. When I gained weight, I became either invisible to most men or I disgusted them. It became very clear: if a man didn't want to sleep with me, I was of no use to him. And a man who disrespects a woman to whom he is not attracted makes it evident that he believes a woman's sole purpose is to be an object of attraction and that conventional attractiveness (thinness) is the only marker of a worthy woman. A woman who does not fulfill her primary obligation of turning him on is therefore not worthy and has no value.

So, in many ways, gaining weight put things into perspective for me. The men who continued to want to have lunch with me or strike up a conversation were interested in me as a human being, the others—the overwhelming majority—ignored me completely. It reminds me of the argument that men and women can't be platonic friends. The thought that this is an accepted fact of life pains me. Are we suggesting that men don't want anything to do with women who don't serve them sexually, either by giving up their bodies or by serving as objects to chase? Sadly, it has been this exact realization that I've encountered far too often in my new body.

Meanwhile, flocks of men are over here complaining about being "friend-zoned," but I'm here to assure you that the "friend zone" is as mythical as Narnia. Really. It doesn't exist. Women are not obligated to show affection to a guy who does her a certain number of favors, or buys dinner, or gives her compliments. Spending time and money is not an investment for which the only return is sex. Women have this funny little thing called free will, where they are actually—believe it or not—allowed to choose who they are sexually attracted to and what they want to do about that attraction. Expecting anything otherwise is straight-up entitlement and reeks of misogyny.

So did being fat make me more of a feminist? Absolutely.

I wholeheartedly believe that how attractive I am to a particular person, or society at large, does not dictate how smart I am, how capable I am, how talented I am, how well I can serve others, or how happy and fulfilled as a human being I can be. I know

that my life and my purpose are so much bigger than being attractive to someone. I am actually able to look back at my weight gain and be grateful for it because it weeded out so many idiots. Now I am sure, without question, that the people in my life, and specifically the men, are here because they want to be and because they love me unconditionally.

Whenever someone tells me she's not a feminist, I feel disheartened, though not completely surprised. After all, 44 percent of women say that the choices women make themselves are a bigger factor in keeping women from achieving full equality with men, rather than discrimination against women (44 percent).[*] Scores of female celebrities have spoken out about how they do not consider themselves feminists, including Kelly Clarkson, Katy Perry, and even Madonna. Take a look at these quotes:

Kelly Clarkson: I wouldn't say feminist—that's too strong. I think when people hear feminist, it's just like, "Get out of my way, I don't need anyone." . . . I love that I'm being taken care of, and I have a man that's an actual leader. . . . I'm not a feminist in that sense.

Katy Perry: I am not a feminist, but I do believe in the strength of women.

Madonna: I'm not a feminist; I'm a humanist.

However, in the years following, they've offered more clarity regarding their responses.

Kelly Clarkson: I was saying that in the past decade, I feel people have associated the word "feminist" with "bitch" and "man-hater" and all these things. And I'm definitely

[*] www.washingtonpost.com/graphics/national/feminism-project/poll

not that girl. That's what I meant by that. Obviously I believe in female equal rights. I'm not an idiot. I'm a female. I believe in equal rights across the board.

Katy Perry: A feminist? Uh, yeah, actually. I used to not really understand what that word meant, and now that I do, it just means that I love myself as a female and I also love men.

Madonna: So, we live in a very ageist society, which means we live in a sexist society because nobody ever gives men shit for how they behave, however old they are. There is no rulebook. As a man, you can date whoever you want. You can dress however you want. You can do whatever you want in any area that you want. But, if you're a woman, there are rules, and there are boundaries.

In an effort to distance themselves from owning a word that has a negative connotation, these women renounced feminism, even though their later words confirmed that they are, in fact, feminists (and thank God, because if Madonna, in all her eighties-armpit-hair and in-your-face sexuality didn't consider herself a feminist, I'm not sure I'd want to live on this planet anymore). As women, I don't think we should be afraid to claim what we are, whether that means being a feminist or being fat. Or both.

I wish we didn't need feminism anymore, but I am a hundred percent certain that we do. Internalized misogyny runs deep and it hurts everyone, including men. Every time we tell a little boy that he can't cry, or that he is gay if he wants to take a dance class (and what's wrong with being gay anyway?), or that he needs to man up and that he's a pussy if he resorts to nonviolence, we are *hurting men.* Championing toxic masculinity is harmful to men, especially in the areas of sexual assault (even though men account for up to 38 percent of sexual assault victims,* they are much less likely than women to report it) and domestic violence, which is typically accepted as a male-on-female problem. It's also important to point out that just because you happen to subscribe to typical gender roles, it doesn't make you a sexist pig or a weak woman. It's perfectly fine for a man to want to provide for his family, and it's perfectly fine for a woman to want to be a stay-at-home mom. However, the reverse is just as okay. Feminism is about choices that every woman has the right to make for herself. When we try to police women's autonomy, sexual or otherwise, that is misogyny.

But this kind of overt policing of women's behavior isn't the only evidence of misogyny—the world is full of microaggressions, too, seemingly small things that add up to a big problem. I was floored recently when a Facebook post of mine went viral. Why? Because it was about a pack of gum . . . kinda.

Because I had a headache, I went into a gas station around nine P.M. in search of Tylenol. As soon as I walked in, the clerk called out, "Hey, sweetheart." I offered him nonverbal acknowledgment and picked up my medicine. When I set it down on the counter, he rang it up, and then I also set a pack of gum on the counter. When he saw the gum, he picked it up, held it to his chest, and said, "You've gotta give me a smile if you want this." But I didn't want to pay for my gum with a smile; I wanted to pay for it with money, so I politely refused, saying, "No thanks, I'll just take the gum." My refusal to play his silly game by smiling on command for him, in exchange for gum that I was willing and eager to pay for, angered him and he immediately started berating me, grumbling about my bad attitude and saying things like, "Man, you can't act like that." He never did ring up my gum, so I put some cash down for the Tylenol and left. When I got home, I was so irritated that I took to Facebook to describe the situation. If I wasn't sure the actual incident is evi-

---

* National Crime Victimization Survey (www.bjs.gov)

dence of why we need feminism, the comment section surely was.

Thousands of people weighed in. The overwhelming majority were women who blasted me, calling me a bitch for not smiling at this man.

> *It's only a smile.*
> *He was trying to cheer you up.*
> *Couldn't you have just humored him?*

I'm sorry, *what*? How could anyone defend someone who refused to do his job until I gave in to his demands (no matter WHAT they were). I'm sure the same people reassuring me that he was only trying to brighten my day would have felt differently if he'd said, "You've gotta go out with me if you want this," or "You've gotta show your tits if you want this." But he didn't—those two scenarios we can recognize as much worse, but really, is a smile THAT big of a deal?

Yes, it is. It is a big deal because it's a microaggression executed by a man who was in a position of power (he had access to what I wanted and the ability to provide or deny it), and he manipulated that power to get something he wanted from me before he would do his job and sell me gum. The BBC filmed an interview with me for their trending segment, and people.com wrote an article about it. All over some gum. (Hot take: it wasn't really about the gum at all.)

A lot of positives came out of this little slice-of-life story, but the worst part was, hands-down, the women tearing me apart at the seams, completely unaware that they don't have to put up with the kind of treatment I received in the gas station, no matter how innocuous it seems. Thousands of women asked why I couldn't just "take a compliment" from this sweet old Southern man. Interestingly enough, two out of three of those assumptions were wrong: the man was neither sweet nor old. In fact, he was younger than me, but I didn't include that detail for the same reason I didn't include the color of his skin—it's irrelevant. I didn't even find it necessary to point out that he spoke in a threatening tone; I thought his actual words were bad enough. People also didn't understand why I viewed this interaction as rife with sexism. The explanation is simple. The clerk would not have required a man to smile before selling him gum, and I feel certain he also would not have required me to smile *for him* if my boyfriend or another man were present with me. Then there were the "victim blamers" (no, I don't really feel victimized over this situation, just pissed) who demanded to know the clerk's side of the story, what I said to him before he asked me to smile, what I was wearing, why I had a headache, etc. They rallied for this anonymous man as though I'd published his first and last name and his mother's address on the Internet. No one seemed to be able to trust that I, as a thirty-two-year-old woman, could possibly have been validated in feeling creeped out, because surely this man was just trying to cheer me up by demanding a smile in exchange for service, even though he never once smiled at me. Do you see any parallels between this and, say, how people react when a woman claims she is raped?

This kind of compliance with microaggressive behaviors is the same reason so many women experience catcalling, and verbal and physical harassment, and accept it as just part of being a woman.

Body-positivity for women without feminism is a futile effort. You cannot truly appreciate your body in the most genuine way until you detach other people's sexual expectations from it. Without feminism, body-positivity is a car without an engine; it loses its (em)power(ment). Do yourselves a favor, ladies: don't be afraid to be a feminist. Feminism is my favorite F-word. Followed by "fat," of course. Can you guess what my third one is? (Hint: it's not "food.")

11

BODY-POSITIVITY DOESN'T PROMOTE OBESITY

There's a whole lot of buzz surrounding body-positivity. It's a frequent flicker in our media these days; the *New York Times* reports on it, celebrities talk about it, and there are entire online communities devoted to it. But what *is* body-positivity?

That's a question I ventured to answer with a YouTube video I made titled *No Body Shame,* after my campaign. Having secured a space and a production company, I set off to find a diverse group of people who could deliver a touching illustration of body-positivity in fewer than three minutes. The only catch? I didn't have any money to pay participants, so I scoured my pool of friends (who would do it for free), looking for people who had experienced the harmful effects of body-shaming and could therefore benefit from body-positivity.

Body-shaming is so pervasive that it took me only fifteen minutes of texting and drawing up a scheduling matrix on a Starbucks napkin to lock down eight volunteers to be part of my video.

My best friend Donna was an obvious recruit. She deals with stereotypes and fetishization daily, but she even encounters

body-shaming from other Koreans because she is an Asian anomaly—she is tall, big-boned, and not skinny. Then there was my old soccer teammate Cristy, who had battled cancer (and won!), but felt self-conscious about the mullet (as she called it) she was left with following treatment. I called my friend Jeff, an amputee who'd lost his leg in a car accident, and he even suggested bringing along his boyfriend, Jason, who enjoys wearing eyeliner and nail polish. My friend Briayna, an overweight, black college student who rocks her natural hair, said she'd be on board, and so did my do-it-with-the-lights-on guy, Peter. Amanda, one of my dancers from the Big Girl Dance Class I teach locally, wanted to join as well, as her tattoos and skinny figure are often the topic of ridicule. And then there was Harley, a burn survivor, who I met during my radio years.

What I ended up with was a remarkable group of human

beings whom I love dearly and were easily relatable to viewers. Then the camera panned to me, and a barrage of outrage followed.

> Are you really comparing yourself to a burn survivor? You're sick.
>
> Please don't tell me you think your life as a fat woman is anything like the injustices gay people face. Give me a break. You've always had your rights.
>
> Are you kidding me? Black and Asian people deserve to feel beautiful because they were born that way, but you weren't BORN fat. Lose weight, you fucking whale.

These are just a few of the reactions the video generated, and in response, I have something earth-shattering to say:

Body-positivity is for *every body,* full stop.

It doesn't matter why we are the way we are. It's irrelevant whether genetics, accidents, diseases, choices, or a combination of all of the above culminated in the body you have right now. Body-positivity maintains that you have every right—hell, an obligation, even—to love the body that you have *right now*. Really. That's it. Period.

So why is it, as body-positivity is making its way into mainstream American conversation, that the willingness to accept the message depends so heavily (no pun intended) on the person who is delivering it?

A new diversified line of Barbie dolls? *It's about time little girls played with dolls who look like them, no matter race, height, or size!* Ashley Graham on the cover of the *Sports Illustrated* swimsuit edition? *Go ahead and show 'em what an average woman's body looks like! Women's Health* dropping the words "bikini body" from future covers? *Ha! Deuces!* Carrie Fisher tweeting a smackdown against those who claimed she hasn't "aged well"? *PREACH.* These are just a few examples of body-positivity making headlines in 2016, and the public is responding in an overwhelmingly positive fashion. Things are finally changing, it seems, and we are truly recognizing the importance of body-positivity in our diet-obsessed, appearance-driven culture.

Until a woman as fat as me talks about it. Then we're just promoting obesity.

I legitimately do not even understand what "promoting obesity" means, but I am accused of it at every turn, no matter what I do. I live my life and someone wags an index finger at me. I wear a two-piece bathing suit on the beach: I'm promoting obesity. I have a television show that focuses on my life: I'm promoting obesity. I smile: I'm promoting obesity. I dance on the Internet: I'm promoting obesity. I'm happy: you guessed it—promoting obesity. When the season two finale of *My Big Fat Fabulous Life* was airing in the States, I was in South Africa doing press for the show there, so Lennie went to a local bar to watch the episode with some friends. As soon as it started, some other male patrons audibly groaned. "What the fuck is this shit? Some bitch on TV because she's fat?" This wasn't the first time he'd come across this, either. When we first started dating, he was telling his good friend about me and mentioned the title of my show. The friend's mood instantly changed. "Well," he'd sighed, "I guess the good thing about fat women is that you don't have to worry about them cheating on you." Lennie then, of course, had to "explain" me, promising his friend that I was awesome, that he would "love me," and that I wasn't "promoting obesity." But for as much as I am questioned about "promoting obesity" by journalists, talk-show hosts, trolls, and even people in my own personal life, I am never given a solution for it. I mean, seriously, if someone believes that living my life is equivalent to spearheading a campaign to encourage people to massively gain weight and become obese, what can I do to change that? What's the alternative?

I could cover up in a one-piece with a swim skirt. Really, I don't have to go to the beach at all; my basement has pretty decent views. I could dedicate myself to feeling like shit all the time (I'm a pro at that!) so no one would ever catch me smiling. I could cancel all my dance classes and quit exercising. Now, we're getting somewhere. If I could manage all these things, there'd be no life to film and put on TV anyway. I did it! I found the solution!

It sounds ridiculous when I put it that way, right? But that's *exactly* what people are implying I do when they criticize me for asserting that, despite weighing close to 400 pounds, I am happy and I have a life worth living. (And, for the record, I once asked an auditorium of seven hundred college students if they watched *My Big Fat Fabulous Life* and supported body-positivity. Nearly all of them raised their hands. Then I asked how many of them had considered purposefully gaining weight to look like me. Can you guess how many kept their hands raised? Zero.) Far from promoting obesity, being body-positive means you have committed yourself to loving and appreciating your body, whatever its current state may be. The advantages of adopting this attitude are not only substantial, but go hand in hand with (if you can believe it) improving your health. Lack of critical thinking may make it easy to dismiss body-positivity as promoting obesity, so let me make clear exactly how I aim to approach my own body-positive lifestyle.

I want to appreciate my body by recognizing its strengths, capabilities, power, and potential. I want to befriend my body by absolving it of perceived flaws—like cellulite, wrinkles, and spider veins—and acknowledge that imperfections are natural and normal. This allows me to embrace my own unique physical beauty. I want to use my body in any way that inspires me, whether it be through art, athletics, or lovemaking. I want to wear whatever I think makes me look good and feel confident—"unflattering" things like midriff shirts and horizontal stripes included. I want to experience everything that life has to offer now, in *this* body, without feeling apologetic about how much space it takes up in public or how aesthetically pleasing other people deem it to be. I never want to hold my body to a fixed set of beauty standards.

I want to have more respect for my body than that, which is also why I want to value it by minimizing any attempts to permanently change or alter it. Sure, I like lipstick and clip-on hair as much as the next gal, but when it comes to plastic surgery, I can do without it. And finally, I want to drown out the noise from fashion magazines, advertisements, and Hollywood, and hone in on the feedback that my body gives me and respond accordingly with nutrition, rest, and exercise. Admittedly, the last goal has been the most challenging one for me to adhere to, and I am far away from mastering it, but I think as a whole, most people would see the worth in following those principles. It just seems kinda . . . healthy, right?

Before you answer that, I should point out that it's a vague question. For a word that dominates so many national and global conversations, the definition of health is hazy, at best. What does it really mean to be healthy in America today? My BMI number is off the charts, well into the "morbidly obese" range, but my blood pressure and my A1C are normal. Am I healthy? My belly fat could scream "unhealthy!" but a snapshot of my exercise habits would suggest the opposite. I have PCOS, which has no cure, but the symptoms can be managed. And, if I am not healthy, who is? Is it the person whose BMI falls into an optimal range? But what if that person smokes? Is he or she still healthy? What about the thin person who lives a sedentary lifestyle and drinks soda every day? Is he or she healthy? How about a person who is only slightly chubby but has sky-high stress levels? The further you go, the blurrier the picture of health becomes.

The dictionary definition of health is: *the condition of being well or free from disease; the condition of being sound in body, mind, or spirit.*

But we tend to emphasize the physical body when we talk about health, forcing other components like mental and emotional health to take a backseat. And we like to interpret health as an absence of undesirable things (heart disease, diabetes, cancer), as opposed to the presence of desirable things (flexibility, endurance, self-confidence). Even though I can't define health any more clearly than the average person, I do know, after my thirty-two years on this Earth, that several things are true: (1) the BMI is bullshit and, therefore, we cannot use size as a fail-proof determinant of health; (2) weight loss is *not* a simple equation of calories in versus calories out; and (3) the pursuit of physical health should not happen at the expense of mental or emotional health.

I entered into a relationship with the BMI scale before I was even aware it existed—remember the doctor who asked my mother to restrict my ice cream and chocolate milk intake? He gave this directive after assessing my BMI. During my teenage years, I referred to the BMI to evaluate exactly how fat I really was, and it told me in an uncomplicated way. All I had to do in that pre-Internet era was find my height on the left side of the chart and then slide my finger to match up with my weight at the top. And just like finding your panty-hose size, colored blocks told me which BMI classification I fit into.

So on the night of my prom, my height of five-two and weight of 145 pounds equaled a BMI of 26.5. The classification: overweight. The recommendation: I would benefit from finding ways to lower my weight, like diet and exercise. What the BMI scale didn't ask me to enter was, well, everything else. Had the BMI scale cared to know, I would have told it that I exercised an average of three hours daily, that I regularly consumed fewer than 2,000 calories per day, and that I passed all the fitness tests in my gym class with flying colors. If I'd known then what I know now, my eighteen-year-old self would have looked the BMI recommendation in the face and said, "Thank you, but no thank you. I'm good." Then I would have put on my tiara and prom princess sash and sauntered right out of the room.

Because what I know now is that the BMI is an unreliable metric of health. No, really, it is, and there's evidence to back this up. First of all, the BMI can't distinguish how much of a person's weight is body fat and how much is muscle and how much is water. This is easy enough to understand, especially in the case of bodybuilders, for example, who are clearly physically fit but get lumped into the "overweight" or "obese" BMI category simply because of their muscles. But a recent study shows that problems with BMI classifications don't stop there—not by a long shot. Obesity researchers examined forty thousand people and uncovered that 29 percent of obese people and 16 percent of morbidly obese people were metabolically healthy; that is to say, they were *not* at risk for type 2 diabetes or heart disease. On the flip side, the study also examined people who were considered in the "normal" weight range and found that thirty percent of them were metabolically unhealthy, meaning they *were* at risk for type 2 diabetes and heart disease. Overall, the data estimates that a staggering 74.9 million Americans are misclassified in some way because their BMI number doesn't match up with their metabolic health.[*] This research completely dismantles the "thin = healthy/fat = unhealthy" construct that is so deeply ingrained in our collective psyche, and if this study had needed photographs to illustrate its points, my best friend, Heather, and I would have made perfect models.

For more than ten years while I was fat, I was in good metabolic health, but in March 2015, when I got a prediabetes diagnosis with an A1C level of 6.4, I felt like I was finally proving negative stereotypes about fat people true (added bonus: I got to do it on national TV!). I was disappointed in myself and fearful

---

[*] www.ncbi.nlm.nih.gov/m/pubmed/26841729

about the very real possibility of developing type 2 diabetes. However, Heather was also diagnosed with prediabetes at the same time, but for some reason her diagnosis didn't feel like a moral failing—not to her or anyone else. Because Heather is skinny, she wasn't racked with the same kind of guilt over developing a metabolic health problem the way I did, and others didn't vilify her for it the same way they did me, either. Meanwhile, I braced myself for a torrent of "See, I told you so's" and similar statements echoing the belief that I'd been lying to myself for all this time and now the day had come: I was fat, and fat meant unhealthy.

It was almost as if fat-shamers rejoiced in my health scare, but all of them were silent when Heather ranted on Facebook about how she couldn't take her low-carb diet one more day and posted a photo of a heaping plate of pasta with the caption #AngelHairDontCare. When I saw that post, I thought two things: (1) Damn, that pasta looks good, and (2) I could never get away with posting this because I'm *actually* fat. I was too afraid to even show my solidarity by liking the post! Luckily, both Heather and I have managed to lower our A1C levels back down to a healthy range, but in another plot twist, I was able to do it in three months (much faster than Heather), and I lost only seventeen pounds in the process, which flies in the face of another widely held belief: that fat people my size must lose hundreds of pounds to see any tangible improvement in their health.

When I posted about my lowered A1C status on social media the night that the doctor's visit episode aired (the same night I was in South Africa and Lennie was defending me at the bar), I expected to receive some Internet high-fives and thumbs-up emojis. What I *didn't* expect was what actually happened: thousands of people who were incensed that I had the gall to share my test results that proved, according to the standards we use to measure metabolic health, that I was simultaneously over 350 pounds and . . . healthy. No one could handle seeing a woman as big as me in a doctor's office being told that my blood pressure was normal and I was out of the woods when it came to prediabetes. No one could handle it because it contradicts what we *want* to believe about the relationship between weight and health. I was accused of manipulating the test results, but even those who believed me were chomping at the bit to remind me that even if I was healthy now, I wouldn't be later, and announcing my "healthy" test results was irresponsible because it led people to think that someone my size could have healthy test results. But *wait*—someone my size *did* have healthy test results. There is absolutely nothing that is misleading or deceptive about that. But more than the hateful skepticism of strangers, I was most bothered by my own need to defend myself. I thought about scanning the results and posting them or asking the doctor to let me take a video of the results in her computer system. Why did I have an insatiable desire to *prove* that I was healthy?

Even before I readily volunteered my life up for public consumption on a reality TV show, I still wanted to be lumped in with the "good fatties." Good fatties are fat people who show remorse for their bodies and who actively strive to correct them. They Instagram pictures of their green juice and their spinach salads and participate in 5Ks out of guilt, instead of pleasure. Bad fatties, on the other hand, are the ones who spend much less time apologizing for—and more time living in—their fat bodies. They don't deem it necessary to wear a Fitbit to demonstrate to others that they keep track of their steps; they just wear a damn Fitbit if they want to. They don't think they owe their health to anyone. Bad fatties are the ones who don't "dress for their bodies"; the ones who don't have any health conditions that contribute to their weight (and they don't care); and the ones who don't take any shit. Truth be told, I exercise because I love to exercise. We should all feel free to do whatever we love, regardless of the size of our bodies. But I don't want to be a "good fatty"; I don't want to tailor what I do and don't do based on satisfying other people. I signed a contract that requires me to share intimate details of my personal life and my health, but I try to release the need for others' approval. Most days, this is easier said than done, but I'm okay with being a work in progress.

One step toward disregarding public approval of my weight is to ignore the BMI scale. Treating the BMI as gospel when it comes to weight and health is bad for all involved. Had the BMI not confirmed the sentiment conveyed in the "Baby Beluga" song from fifth grade, maybe I never would have developed such a bad body image to begin with; I can't be sure, of course, but I certainly could have done without an arbitrary measurement reinforcing the ideas that young girls struggle with enough on their own. And as it stands, the BMI is still the conclusive way for health insurance companies to figure out how to offer financial discounts or penalties to policyholders, for employers to offer incentives and rewards based on BMI-assessed weight loss, and how doctors diagnose people as overweight or obese. (By the way, the American Medical Association now officially recognizes obesity as a disease, even though the association's council on science and public health disagreed, for the exact reason that the BMI as a diagnostic tool is simplistic and flawed.)*

Even if we could accurately diagnose obesity as a disease with a quick and easy tool and then prescribe weight loss as treatment, how would we go about helping people institute that in their daily lives? As long as I've been alive, the advice for weight loss has consisted of two main tenets: eat less and exercise more. This may seem like sound advice on the surface, but we are

---

* www.nytimes.com/2013/06/19/business/ama-recognizes-obesity-as-a-disease.html

doing people a disservice if we lead them to believe that weight loss is the inevitable result of an equation as straightforward as calories in versus calories out, plus 30 minutes of exercise.

First of all, focusing only on calories consumed and calories burned tells us nothing about what *kind* of calories they are. All calories are not created equal. Two hundred calories from soda and 200 calories from vegetables are not the same thing because the human body is a complex system that regulates energy balance through different processes, and different calorie sources have different effects on hunger, hormones, and energy expenditure.* My dietician, Julie, urges me to stop calorie counting and start listening to my body. Women who have insulin resistance (a lovely side effect of PCOS) don't process carbs like people whose bodies regulate insulin properly. This is why women with PCOS are told to eat foods that are low in the glycemic index (low GI)—these foods help prevent insulin spikes. When Julie first introduced me to this idea, she asked me to listen to my body and think about how I felt after I ate a carb-heavy meal (like fettuccine Alfredo, for example). When I took her advice and became receptive to my body, I found that my favorite foods left me feeling sluggish and sleepy. No calorie counting or moral judgment about "bad food" was required for me to realize the benefit of trading refined carbs for protein more often than not. I don't have to say "pasta la vista" to Italian restaurants; I just need to pay attention to how they make me feel and order accordingly.

The takeaway: PCOS complicates more for me than can be fixed by simply counting calories, and to believe in a diet myth like "weight loss is calories in, calories out" completely dismisses the presence of diseases and disorders (think Cushing's syndrome, thyroid disorders, and Hashimoto's disease) that play a huge role in how our bodies gain and lose weight. If weight loss

---

* www.theatlantic.com/health/archive/2014/06/calories-are-out/372690

depended solely on the amount of calories consumed and the amount of exercise completed, I would have lost 300 pounds back in 2011, not 100. And none of us would have that friend who eats junk, never exercises, and stays rail thin. Weight loss, just like our bodies, is not as simple as we are made to believe.

Now, don't get me wrong; I *have* made a concerted effort to stop allowing numbers on a scale to run (and ruin) my life, but I don't think weight loss is inherently evil. I think where we get it wrong so much of the time is that we've convinced ourselves that weight loss is a behavior, but let's get it straight: weight loss is NOT a behavior. A behavior is opting for a high-protein meal instead of a carb-heavy one. A behavior is loading up a dinner plate with vegetables or taking a walk around the block to get your blood flowing and your heart rate up. We can control behaviors, but as I know all too well, we can't control weight loss the same way. We can't just snap our fingers and demand that the scale reflect the five miles we ran or the liter of water we drank. The problem is that we think we can, so when the scale doesn't give you a gold star in the form of a lower number, we all completely lose our shit. I'm totally for engaging in behaviors that make you feel good, but I cannot, and will never again, support weight loss at all costs or weight loss at the expense of mental and emotional health.

When I was on my weight-loss kick, my eating disorder (bulimia) returned, and I'm sure that wasn't the only form of disordered eating I would have been diagnosed with at the time. Eating disorders are a mental illness, and anorexia has the highest mortality rate of any mental illness. No matter how much emphasis we place on the scale, I could never look at photos of myself then and now and decide I was healthier before. Yes, in 2011, I weighed only 229 pounds, but I was in the grip of an eating disorder as well as depression and anxiety. Now, I am over 350 pounds, but I am so much more emotionally and mentally well, which in the big picture is so much more important to me. A smaller body means nothing to me if I am mentally or emotionally sick—my goal is to strive for balance in all three areas.

The reason that I, like so many others, was readily willing to sacrifice my mental and emotional health for the sake of being thin(ner) is in no small part due to weight stigma and fat-shaming. I know, I know, not everyone believes that fat-shaming is a thing, but, trust me, it is a thing, and we are finding out now more than ever just how harmful weight stigma is to those who experience it. The *Journal of Health Psychology* found that obese women experience an average of three incidents of stigmatization each day.* So, what do these experiences look like? They can be experiences that happen between people socially, like when I am ridiculed on an online dating site and called a "whale" (BTW, I *really* wish people would get more creative with their insults). It can happen in the workplace, too. Fat people are assumed to be lazy and lacking in willpower; these undesirable qualities can in turn prevent fat people from getting jobs or promotions. In the medical field, many fat people experience such severe weight stigma that they never want to go back to the doctor, period. This can be annoying (but mostly benign), like a doctor in Korea who swore my weight was a contributing factor to my earache, or it can be much worse; healthcare professionals frequently misdiagnose, mistreat, and sometimes straight up deny medical treatment to fat people.

In September 2015, I responded to an online video titled *Dear Fat People* with my own video (which has more than 17.7 million views on Facebook). In the original video, a woman claims that "fat-shaming isn't a thing" and suggests that if making people feel bad enough about their weight encourages them

---

* www.minnpost.com/second-opinion/2016/01/obese-women-experience-much-more-negative-social-stigma-previously-thought-st

to lose some, then she's "okay with that." But studies show over and over that making people feel bad about their weight has the opposite effect: it causes them to gain more weight.* Nothing will send a fatty for the bottom of an ice cream bowl faster than demoralizing them on the basis of their body size. I'm half kidding, but it's true—fat people who are made to feel bad about their weight are more likely to avoid the doctor (guilty, from ages eighteen to twenty-two, coincidentally when I began gaining weight) and less likely to engage in healthy habits. This is exactly why I started Big Girl Dance Class (where you don't have to be big in body, just big in spirit). What I had was tons of local girls who loved to dance but didn't feel like they had a safe space to do it. One of my BGDC members is actually a girl I danced with in high school, and even though she's a dance teacher now by profession, she was so embarrassed about her weight gain that she refused to dance in any other class or in public. It's the same thing I suffered through in college when I had an outright fear of going to the gym, especially after one of my trainers spent the whole time I was on the treadmill critiquing the butt of the girl in front of me, saying, "Man, she shouldn't be wearing those shorts!" I could only imagine what he was thinking about me. The fear of being ostracized is what kept me in my darkened apartment, drinking alone and ordering pizza. And gaining more weight.

Call me a crazy skeptic, but it certainly appears like we've been fed massive lies about weight and health for a long time. But why would this happen? Who would benefit from perpetuating this misinformation? Well, the diet industry, for one. In 2012, Americans spent over $60 billion on dieting, including gym memberships, weight-loss surgeries, and diet books and

* www.washingtonpost.com/news/to-your-health/wp/2014/09/11/fat-shaming -doesnt-work-a-new-study-says

pills. And as hard as it is, we can actually drop out of the diet industry. This feels a bit like breaking up with a lifelong boyfriend, as it's been part of most women's lives, well, forever. Approximately 81 percent of ten-year-olds are afraid of being fat. Let that sink in. Ten-year-olds! Forty percent of girls in grades one through three want to be thinner.* This is insanity, but you *can* opt out of it, and choose to focus on your real, holistic health instead. Imagine what would happen if we quit shelling out our money because we hate our bodies and instead put our energy into loving our bodies and showing ourselves compassion. This is exactly what the HAES (Health at Every Size) movement, created by Dr. Linda Bacon, intends to do. As her website (lindabacon.org) says, "She shifts the focus from *weight* to *well-being*, giving doctors, dietitians, therapists, and people of all shapes the tools for achieving better fitness, health and even happiness—all without dieting." In her book, *Health at Every Size: The Surprising Truth About Your Weight,* she expertly busts dogmatic myths about the correlation between weight and health, but just reading this information from pioneers like Dr. Bacon isn't enough. We have to believe it. We have to *live it.*

When we prioritize caring for our bodies over changing our bodies, we can achieve a better balance of physical, mental, and emotional health. I'm not here to say that being fat is better for you than being fit, or that there are no risks associated with being the size I am. But I am here to tell you that hating your body will never get you anywhere faster than loving it will, and that we are not required to spend our lives investing in an industry that sets us up for failure.

Receiving mixed messages from media certainly doesn't help, either. The same women's magazines that are introducing body-positivity into their issues still include full-page advertisements of the latest diets, meal-replacement plans, cleanses,

---

* www.nationaleatingdisorders.org/get-facts-eating-disorders

or pills aimed to whip our bodies into shape. These "fixes" may work in the short term, but they are successful (for the diet industry) in the long term precisely because they *don't* work. Between one and five years later, a whopping 95 percent of dieters will regain the weight they lost[*] (again, guilty). Crop tops and short shorts are almost always seen on slender women (or maybe a perfectly proportioned size 14 model, if we're lucky), while we legitimately fat women are relegated to guessing at what a garment might look like on us if we're fortunate enough to have it come in our size. Media and advertisements are powerful, and the message they sell women is simple: thinness equals happiness. If we are fat, sure, we could be smart or successful in one area of our life, but to truly lasso our Hollywood ending and have it all, we need to be thin. How many times have you seen brilliant, talented, and successful women who have become famous shrink through dieting or surgery to a shadow of their former selves only to yo-yo for the rest of their careers? I'm tired of seeing plus-size women who assert they are happy, healthy, and confident one minute turn into spokeswomen for diet products the next. When will we stop insisting that inside a fat woman exists a thinner, better version of herself just trying to claw her way past the belly flab to get out? There is no thin woman inside of *me*. I am fat through and through, and the only reason I was able to transform from a miserable fat woman to a happy fat woman with a successful career and a whole lot of love in her life is because I decided to quit waiting to lose weight and become the woman I knew I could be right now.

Having said all this, I want to emphasize something that I

---

[*] Grodstein, F., Levine, R., Spencer, T., Colditz, G. A., & Stampfer, M. J. "Three-year follow-up of participants in a commercial weight loss program. Can you keep it off?" *Archives of Internal Medicine* (1996), 156 (12), 1302–06; Neumark-Sztainer D., Haines, J., Wall, M., & Eisenberg, M. "Why does dieting predict weight gain in adolescents? Findings from project EAT-II: a 5-year longitudinal study." *Journal of the American Dietetic Association* (2007) 103 (3), 448–55.

think is even more important: your health is no one else's business. Just because someone can see weight on a person and that leads them to believe that person is unhealthy does not mean anyone has the right to make another person feel shitty about their body or their health. Weight bias is the last socially acceptable form of prejudice in our society, and it's getting old, y'all.

Why can't we just support each other gently and lovingly? No one has an obligation to seek out a particular level of health. We don't all have to be triathletes and we don't all have to eat gluten-free. We are allowed to live happily in the bodies that we have and do the best we can. I don't understand it when people demand that we seek "the best possible body" we could have.

Why? What if I'd rather read a book or spend time with my hypothetical children or whatever? We don't all have to chase an ideal of physical perfection to be deemed worthy or acceptable. I do love to exercise, whether I am fat or not, but I don't think it's fair to tell a fat person they have to exercise any more than we tell a thin person that. Health is more than a number. It is more than the shape and size of our bodies. And it is up to each person to decide what health means for them and how they want to pursue it.

And that begs the question: how do *I* want to pursue it? In one word: holistically. Right now I feel grateful to be in good metabolic health, but especially because I have PCOS, I will have to remain hypervigilant of my weight to stave off further complications. Even though I'm not prediabetic now, that doesn't mean I'll never be at risk again, and that's not something I take lightly. While I may be much healthier than the average person assumes I am just based on my size, I'm only thirty-two, and I don't know what forty-two or fifty-two holds; but I vow to be present in my life and in my health and tweak accordingly. I'd love to be around for some grandchildren. Instead of focusing on the scale, I want to focus on healthy behaviors that I know will help me feel better and promote my overall well-being. Behaviors I want to strive for include taking all of my PCOS medications, using my C-PAP machine to remedy my sleep apnea (an obesity party favor that I'm not a fan of), eating mindfully, and exercising regularly. And weekly appointments with my therapist don't hurt, either. If I were to master these behaviors, or even significantly improve on them, it's quite possible that I may lose some weight without even "trying," but I am quite certain I will never be "thin" (i.e., under 250 pounds) ever again, and that's okay. Your love for yourself does not have to be conditional. Forget my future husband—I take you, Whitney, to have and to hold from this day forward; for better or worse; for richer or poorer; in sickness and in health; to love and to cherish all the days of my life. *This* is my solemn vow. I mean, seriously, if we're expected to promise that stuff to our partners, don't we deserve it for ourselves?

Hypothetical dream wedding between myself and myself aside, if I woke up tomorrow at my old goal weight of 130 pounds, sure, there would be some good that would come of it. I'd have way more clothing options, and the instant approval of most people who pass me on the street. I would have an Olympic-size dating pool (if I wanted to dip my toe in). Hell, I might even be able to hold a cup between my legs in the car. Those would all be fun things. But if I'm honestly weighing the two (no pun intended), there are more important things that I wouldn't have. I wouldn't have a living record of my misery or happiness. I wouldn't have skin that shows the battle scars of the woman I fought to become. I wouldn't have the same confidence, pride, and unconditional love for myself that I gained only from going through hell and back and by learning to live in this body.

So, dear fat people, what I want to say to you is this: You are loved. You are worthy, and you are capable of so much more than you think. And a number, whether it be on a scale or a measuring tape, cannot quantify the value that you have; it cannot count all the ways that this world needs you; it cannot define your health or project your success. *Your weight does not measure your worth.*

And if I can give only one piece of advice, it is this: be visible.

The first time I really claimed my space and demanded that people see me was during that boudoir photo shoot more than two and a half years ago. That moment changed my life, and I have never looked back. I've worked hard to build a career, however, I know I have the privilege of being appealing to a mainstream audience. Yes, I'm huge, but I have a medical condition that makes other people much more comfortable because they feel they can use it to justify my weight. I have tattoos, but they're small and easily hidden so as not to offend; I'm white and I'm able-bodied and therefore consistent with the American majority; I have a (marginally) conventionally attractive face, an adorable family, and hilarious friends. Add in dancing skill, a viral video, a heartfelt message and voila—it was the perfect storm. However, I know there are women out there facing greater challenges than I am who *stay* slaying. They aren't necessarily the ones garnering media attention, either, and that sucks. Every kind of marginalized person deserves media representation and the only way to strive for that is to make people notice you—in your real life and on user-controlled platforms like the Internet. I don't care what color you are, how many tattoos you're covered in, why you're fat, if you're able-bodied or not, whether you're an hourglass or an apple—keep dancing. But do be warned: making yourself visible also invites vulnerability. When you let people in, that includes those who love you unconditionally, the "Sarah Lynns" of the world, and everyone in between. Is it worth it? You bet.

When you risk a lot, you gain a lot. And when I started taking risks, I found both my bedroom and my life illuminated, and I discovered that the things I'd always wanted were *here*, right beside me—I just couldn't see them when I was spinning in circles in the dark. You are the *only* one who has the power to flip the switch, but body-positivity is an undertaking that has to be lived day in and day out. Sure, you'll have some sudden lightbulb moments and instantaneous inspiration here and there, but the road to shame-free bliss happens largely in the dark. You have to advance toward a light switch that *you can't see* but trust that you'll ultimately get there. That means slogging through the gloom—wearing that bikini, talking to that love interest, taking that dance class, prioritizing your self-worth over your "attractiveness"—all without being able to pinpoint exactly where you are in the process. But if you keep challenging yourself; if you remember that confidence is a product of action and not the other way around; and if you keep moving forward, one day—sooner than you think—it'll happen. Boom. You'll find the switch.

Lights on.

Acknowledgments

A thousand thank-yous to Ballantine Books for (1) agreeing to publish my book and (2) for making me feel so good about it in the process. To my editor, Sara Weiss, thank you for your patience in dealing with an incredibly anxious and high-strung first-time author (that's me!). Your steadfast encouragement was so appreciated and so necessary. To my literary agent, Mollie Glick, thank you for being in my corner and advocating for me every step of the way. This dream would not have become a reality without you! To my project manager, superwoman, and friend, Rennie Dyball . . . sister, thank you for your constant guidance, gentle pushes, and endless reassurances. You made me believe I could write a book—in four months!—because you believed in me and because you held my hand through every single stage. I could never have done this without you (like, literally, I'd still be on chapter 1). I could never repay you for all the time and emotional energy you poured into this project and into me. I am fortunate to have worked with such a brilliant, beautiful, remarkable woman as you and to be able to call you a friend. So many thanks always to my manager, Michael DeFosse, to whom I owe basically everything. Thank you for everything you do, and have always done for me.

A huge thanks to all the supporters of No Body Shame and fans of *My Big Fat Fabulous Life.* Thank you for letting me into your life.

Thank you to all of the people who enrich my life every minute just by being in it—Heather, Donna, Todd, Tal, Ashley,

Buddy, Leslie, and Lennie—I love you. Can't imagine this world without you.

And thanks to my family . . . to my mother, my father, and my brother, Hunter, for being the most amazing, supportive, loving human beings on the planet. Hunter, thank you for being the big brother I always wanted. Mommy, thank you for being who I want to be when I grow up—your wit, humor, and beauty are unparalleled. And, Daddy, thank you for teaching me how to be strong. You'll always be my coach.

About the Author

WHITNEY WAY THORE's viral YouTube series "A Fat Girl Dancing" thrust her into the spotlight and sparked a global conversation about body image, leading her to found the No Body Shame campaign to help people of every variety love and live their lives free of shame. As a body-positive activist and self-love advocate, Whitney has appeared on dozens of national and international television programs and continues to garner attention from media outlets worldwide. Whitney currently stars in TLC's hit reality show *My Big Fat Fabulous Life*, which showcases her family and friends, her dance career, and her life with PCOS. When she's not on TV, Whitney keeps busy by speaking at universities, writing, and dancing. She lives in Greensboro, North Carolina, with her two cats, Henchi and Wanda.

nobodyshame.com
Facebook.com/whitney.thore
@WhitneyWay
Instagram.com/whitneywaythore
YouTube.com/user/nobodyshame

About the Type

This book was set in Legacy, a typeface family designed by Ronald Arnholm (b. 1939) and issued in digital form by ITC in 1992. Both its serifed and unserifed versions are based on an original type created by the French punch-cutter Nicholas Jenson in the late fifteenth century. While Legacy tends to differ from Jenson's original in its proportions, it maintains much of the latter's characteristic modulations in stroke.